Advance Praise for *It's Only an Opinion*

"Hank's book is an interesting and educational romp through some of the important real estate appraisal experiences in his long and illustrious career. This book should be required reading, and get continuing education credit for freshman appraisers—both residential and commercial. It is a great proxy for experience in general business and contracting with expert witnesses. Where else could an aspiring expert witness spend a few fun hours and learn about:

- Important professional associations and designations
- Intangible assets; statistics and probability
- Daubert and Khumo tests for expertness in court
- The nature of Florida wetlands
- A ton of definitions normally treated in courses
- Methods of business appraisers
- 'Across the fence' valuations
- Collecting one's fee from disgruntled clients
- New, senior living centers like CCRCs
- Stories behind prominent Atlanta real estate landmarks
- Aspects of getting into and retiring from appraisal firms

You also will learn colorful new terms of speech such as:

'Even a bass wouldn't get in much trouble if he learned to keep his mouth shut.'

'Growing chickens are machines to transform corn into chicken and fertilizer.'

'It's much more important to be believed than to be right when you are an expert witness.'

He offers great advice to prospective litigating clients. My favorite anecdote is the one about Continuing Care Retirement Communities;

all appraisers should read this one. Hank is illuminating while teaching in this book and not afraid to help us readers by sharing mistakes anybody could have made and learned from."

—James D. "Jim" Vernor is Chairman Emeritus of Real Estate, Georgia State University, in Atlanta, Georgia, where he served on the full-time faculty from 1974 through 1997. He has a BBA, MBA and PhD all from the University of Wisconsin, with majors in real estate and finance. He holds the MAI and is currently serving a third term as a member of the DeKalb County Georgia Board of Tax Assessors.

"Hank is a master storyteller. He takes the esoteric topic of appraisal and weaves it into an entertaining and informative memoir of his life's work. I couldn't put it down!"

—Sandra Zayac, public finance attorney
Partner at Arnall, Golden & Gregory, LLP

"Hank and I were to testify in the same case on the behalf of the same client. I was up one day, and Hank was testifying the next day. The cross-examining attorney asked me: 'Why are you getting paid only $150/hour, whereas Mr. Wise, who is testifying tomorrow, gets paid more than twice as much?' I turned to the jury and said: 'You will find out tomorrow!'"

—Joe Kusmik, independent appraiser

"Hank always used to give us appraisers praise in the form of an 'AttaBoy!' (or 'AttaGirl!'). We were also constantly reminded that even one 'AwwShiiit!' error could wipe away a whole mountain of AttaBoys. For Hank's book, covering a life already well lived with many more chapters to come, I can only wholeheartedly yell ATTABOY!"

—Andy Sheppard, principal at Pritchett, Ball & Wise, Inc.

"Great recaps and insight into extremely difficult and unique appraisal assignments!"

—Carl Schultz, past president of The Appraisal Institute and of the National Association of Realtors and a past member of the Appraisal Standards Board.

"Henry J. Wise's book, *It's Only an Opinion*, has provided us a new perspective on the 'mystery' that is an appraisal. From caves to the Everglades his stories shed light on the unique role that an appraiser plays in the economy."

—Rajeev Dhawan, Director, Economic Forecasting Center
—J. Mack Robinson, College of Business – Georgia State University

"It's a fun read from the self-deprecating and humorous cover to the final benediction. A tough subject well presented by an accomplished and experienced professional."

—William C. Tyler, past chairman of Tyler Yates Financial Group, Atlanta, GA and a retired CBRE executive after 25 years. Author of *Critical Thinking: A Primer*, A Tyler family memoir.

IT'S ONLY AN *Opinion*

AN APPRAISER IN COURT

HENRY J. WISE
EXPERT WITNESS

OLD STONE PRESS

It's Only An Opinion: An Appraiser In Court
By Henry J. Wise

Published by Old Stone Press
an imprint of J. H. Clark & Associates, Inc.
Louisville, Kentucky 40207 USA
www.oldstonepress.com

Copyright © 2019 by Henry J. Wise

All rights reserved.

For information about special discounts for bulk purchases or autographed copies of this book, please contact J. H. Clark, Old Stone Press at john@oldstonepress.com or the author, Henry J. Wise at hjwise1939@gmail.com

Library of Congress Control Number: 2018963428
ISBN: 978-1-938462-35-1

Published in the United States

[Please note, although the stories in this book are based on the author's actual appraisal experiences, he has protected the confidentiality of his clients' information. Any dollar amounts cited in this book are for illustrative purposes only, and do not reflect real dollars associated with any legitimate appraisal assignment.]

Contents

Dedication

This book is dedicated to the memory of James Hill Pritchett, MAI, SRPA, SRA. Jim was my mentor, boss, partner and great friend from the time I met him in 1984 until his death in 2002. Along this path I met many other guides, teachers and friends, including Joe W. Ball, MAI, who served as President of Pritchett, Ball & Wise, Inc., for much of my career. I am also indebted to Danny White, MAI, who was a partner in Pritchett, Ball and White, Inc., which was the firm I joined and later became Pritchett, Ball and Wise, Inc. I am pleased that the firm still exists, although there is no longer a Pritchett, Ball or Wise left to answer the phone. The legacy persists under the capable guidance of George Petkovich, MAI, and Andy Sheppard, MAI. I hired Andy out of his graduating class at GSU, which may be the best thing I ever did to further the appraisal profession. As I write this, Andy is presently the President of the Atlanta Chapter of the Appraisal Institute.

Acknowledgements

This book would not exist if it were not for my wife, Shelley Beth Yeatman, who told me that if my stories were ever to interest anyone, I had to write them down. I would be remiss if I didn't also mention and thank Jim Vernor, Ph.D., MAI, who has been my teacher, friend and colleague throughout this interesting journey. Two of my appraisal colleagues, Craig Huber, MAI, and Brad Carter, CRE, MAI, were encouraging early readers of parts of the book, as were Rajeev Dhawan, Ph.D., Director of the Economic Forecasting Center of Georgia State University and John Edwin Smith, author and military historian. I also wish to thank my niece Ranate Patrick and Earle Clowney, Ph.D. for their proofreading and editorial suggestions. I had no idea that I had left my participles dangling for all the world to see.

Chapter 1: The Consequence of an Error

I was driving back from the Carroll County Courthouse with that sick and hollow feeling in my stomach, wondering why in the name of heaven I had ever gotten into this profession and how I was going to tell my new partners that I had probably just cost us a lawsuit because I had screwed up in court.

The case was a confirmation hearing. I now know that when a lender forecloses on a loan against real estate in Georgia, he or she must "bid" the property in a public auction at the local courthouse. If the debtor owes more than the "fair market value" of the property and the loan is "recourse" debt, the lender can go after the borrower's other assets to make up the difference.

The usual process is that a lender will hire an appraiser to determine the market value of the asset at the time of the foreclosure, and the lender will bid the appraised market value at the auction. The debtor's protection is that the court must "confirm" that the lender's bid (which was based on the appraiser's opinion) was at or above market value before the creditor can claim the balance of the loan from the debtor's other assets. If the court determines that the lender paid less than market value, the court will not confirm the sale.

I had been hired by the attorney for a private lender to appraise a several-hundred-acre tract of land on which the lender was foreclosing because the borrower had defaulted. In this case the borrower was a noted defaulter. His general business strategy was to buy a large, timbered tract in a semirural or exurban area, usually with a very modest down payment and substantial owner financing. Early in the process, often during the "due diligence" period, he would sell off all the merchantable timber, any cows that may have been on the property, a tractor or two and, if he was lucky, some higher value components from the larger parcel. The "seller" seldom received much more than the original down payment and the grief of a lawsuit and a clouded title. The less the selling party knew about his property, the better for this "buyer," but there are lots of absentee owners of large tracts of undeveloped land who have never seen what they own, so this crook's business plan worked for quite a while.

When I took the assignment in the spring of 1990, I had never heard of a "confirmation hearing," and I didn't know that I would probably have to defend my appraisal in court. I didn't learn that I would be a witness until sometime in the fall of 1992, about two years after I had finished the appraisal. But what is the worry?

I reviewed the file. The subject of the appraisal was about 150 acres of vacant land that bordered an eight-lane, limited access bypass and a well-trafficked secondary road near a golf course. The highest and best use of about 20 acres that constituted the frontage along the secondary road (to a depth of about 300 feet) was for potential commercial development, and the balance was for potential residential development. I had valued the potential commercial land at about $40,000 per acre and the potential residential land at about $15,000 per acre.[1] I had comparable sales to support the value for each type of land use, and I thought I had done a reasonable job of coming to a credible opinion of value. I went into the hearing with only moderate trepidation.

It wasn't until I was under cross-examination that I learned that I had gotten a fact wrong. The copy of the property survey that my client had given me turned out to be only a Xerox copy of the original plat, and my copy excluded one course of the frontage dimension. Consequently, I misstated the size of the potential commercial property by about 75' of frontage. The other side, the debtor's attorney, had a certified copy of the original plat and showed the court that I had understated the "commercial" acreage by about ½ acre. I can still see the judge using his

---

[1] *Please note that the dollars I cite in this book or in the article are for illustration purposes only, and do not reflect any actual revenues associated with any actual appraisal assignment. I still have a responsibility to my clients of the confidentiality of their financial information, even once the assignment is concluded.*

fingers as a protractor and hear him saying that he thought that I had missed those 72.6 feet of frontage. He asked me: "Mr. Wise, does that make any difference in your appraised value?"

I had already testified that the appraisal was based on the potential land use. I whipped out my trusty HP-12C and calculated that a change of ½ acre from potential residential land to potential commercial land caused a value difference of about $15,000 on a $2,750,000 appraisal, or an error of less than ½ of 1%. It was then that the judge told me that the law required that the lender cannot bid less than "fair market value" by as little as $1.00, and that he could not confirm the sale. He dismissed the case without prejudice, which meant that the lender could go through the process of re-bidding the property and holding another confirmation hearing, but all the time and cost up to this point were wasted.

Pritchett, Ball & Wise, Inc., and our errors and omissions (E&O) insurance carrier had to pay back our appraisal fee plus about $25,000 in the retaining lawyer's fees and related court costs to avoid being sued. I don't believe we ever got another job from that attorney, but I learned an extremely valuable lesson. I learned that an appraiser can't get into any trouble for an error in judgment, but he surely can experience an embarrassing and expensive screw up if he gets a fact wrong. I learned that it is my job to check on all the facts and not to trust anyone, especially my own client!

Part of what it means to be an independent expert is to look at the original plats or recorded surveys, measure the buildings yourself or work from certified "as built" plans. We must undertake all the due diligence efforts that make it clear that we have done what another responsible professional would typically do to ascertain the facts about the asset we are appraising. I had made my factual error about the total length of the front footage almost two years before I discovered my error.

Had I discovered the mistake before the lender bid in the property at the courthouse steps, there would have been no harm, no foul, other than a little embarrassment on my part. Had I discovered the error after the auction, but before the hearing, the lender could have re-bid the property and rescheduled the hearing, and the cost would have been a few hundred dollars for the required legal notices. As it was, we were out of pocket about $3,500 to pay the appraisal fee back, another $5,000 for the deductible on our E&O policy. Even today, over 35 years later, whenever I begin to lean on my laurels or brag on my career, I hear the quiet voice of memory reminding me of that ride back to the office from the Carroll County Courthouse.

At its very best, an appraisal is only an opinion. Most of the time it is an opinion about the value of something, usually the value of an interest in real estate or the value of a business or of a part of a business, or of personal property, such as books, jewelry, fine art, machinery and equipment or, sometimes, an opinion about the highest and best use of something or about the supply and demand factors that affect the value of something.

If an appraisal opinion is to be useful it must be credible. That means it must be worthy of being believed. It must be an independent opinion. It must be free from bias and free from any conflict of interest, which means it must be independent from anyone who has an interest in the outcome of whatever contemplated action motivated the request for the appraisal. Finally, it must be a well-reasoned opinion. A reader should be able to follow the appraiser's reasoning from the facts through the economics to the appraiser's conclusion. "Trust me" is not an acceptable basis for an appraisal.

Chapter 2: Becoming an Appraiser

Like almost everyone else I have been listening to and watching the politicians, pundits and economists working through the problems of pricing what we now call "toxic assets." The economy has not figured out a way to set "value" when buyers and sellers are not buying and selling.

Over the last 35 years I have earned my living by forming an opinion about value under exactly these circumstances. My appraiser colleagues and I labor in obscurity, filling a tiny niche in the demands of the economy by stating an opinion about what value the market would set on a specific interest in a specific tangible or intangible asset as of a specific date, if only the market could work. To the extent that the world believed my opinions, either based on my powers of persuasion or out of abject necessity, I played a useful role in the society and managed to earn a living.

I am not suggesting that appraisers can solve the economic crisis. Appraisals are useful only if they are believed, and no one is likely to, nor should they, believe my opinions about the value of the tangled, financial instruments clogging up the banking system. However, now that serious people are paying attention to the types of problems that have made up my working world, it might be useful to see how an appraiser thinks about "value," especially about the value of a variety of unusual assets under unusual circumstances.

I drifted into this peculiar part craft, part profession with no more knowledge of what it meant to be an appraiser than I believe is known by the general population at large. I had met residential appraisers as a part of the process when I bought my houses, but other than "$350 for three comps" I had no idea what it was that they did. I first discovered commercial appraisal in the semirural town of Conyers, Georgia, in 1982. My now deceased first wife, Linda, and I lived in an "in-town"

Georgia farmhouse that had been built in 1887 on the secondary main street. We were the third owners. The house was zoned as commercial property, which meant that I could indulge a long-held fantasy of having a wine and cheese shop in my front room. I thought that I knew a little about wine when I opened the shop, and I was exactly right, I knew a little about wine.

Linda taught at Rockdale High School, where she was already well on her way to becoming a legend. She taught senior English, but her great strength was as the director of the theater. Holly Hunter was her student, as were Hunter Bell, Jeff Edgerton, Keith Thomas, Victor Smith, Bill Johns, Ken Cosby, Debbie Bisno, Henry Hylan Scott and, eventually, many other kids who have gone on to professional careers in the performing arts. If she had only been the football coach instead of the drama coach, my retirement would be much more secure.

Together we went to the Broadway opening of "Parade" to see Jeff Edgerton, who had been one of Linda's students at Woodward Academy. Later I would go to the Broadway opening of "Title of Show," which was written by and starred Hunter Bell, one of Jeff's Woodward classmates. Hunter was nominated for a 2009 Tony Award. In 2006, following her death, Linda was inducted into the Hall of Fame for teachers of theater by the Educational Theatre Association (EdTA). Jerry D. Smith, one of Linda's protégés who followed her into teaching, was the national president of EdTA the year she was inducted. Linda and I had 38 years together, and she still hangs out over my shoulder most of the time.

After Linda had taught 23 years in Georgia's public schools, Woodward Academy, the largest private school in the continental US, asked her to head their theater program. One year's commuting was enough, and it became time to sell. I called a residential appraiser friend from the Conyers Rotary Club. He told me that since my house was actually a commercial property, I needed to talk with a commercial appraiser. He gave me several names.

I had fished with Joe W. Ball, MAI, as a part of the Conyers Bass

Pros, but I had no idea what he did for a living. Joe, who was a partner at Pritchett, Ball & White, Inc. (much later to become my own firm, Pritchett, Ball & Wise, Inc.), said that he wanted almost $1,800 to look at the property and give me an oral opinion. I told Joe that I had already bought the house once and didn't intend to pay for it again. I only needed to know a reasonable selling price. Joe explained that there was a big difference between a residential appraiser and a commercial appraiser starting with how much money commercial appraisers were paid. This was the first time I heard the term "commercial appraiser."

I had come to Georgia in 1961 to attend Emory University's Graduate School in Political Science, and, following a year as an instructor at the University of North Carolina, Charlotte, I moved back to teach at West Georgia College in Carrollton, about 35 miles west of Atlanta. By 1968 I knew that I would not make a life of teaching college, and my new bride and I moved to Atlanta with the Georgia Municipal Association, where I was responsible to the city officials for the quality and scope of local government training.

Eventually, I became responsible for all technical assistance to the cities and counties in Georgia, which – I felt – qualified me to begin a local government consulting practice. In short order I learned that you had to be careful what you name yourself. "Wise and Associates, Inc.," what could be wrong with that? The letters came addressed to Wise Ass. Inc., and, for the next 18 years, "Wise Ass Inc." is what it was.

From colonial days through the passage of the Financial Institution Reform, Recovery and Enforcement Act of 1989 (FIRREA), if you said you were an appraiser and if anyone paid any money for or attention to your opinion, you were an appraiser. We were a completely unregulated profession. Governments worried about the competence and honesty of plumbers, electricians, lawyers, doctors and, following the Great Depression, accountants; but appraisers were never believed to play an important enough role in the economy to warrant regulation. Real Estate brokers and agents, barbers, beauticians and waste water plant operators had to be state licensed, but not appraisers.

About the only assurance of appraiser ethics and competence available to the public came from the professional associations. The oldest and most prestigious – at least in the field of commercial real estate appraisal – was the American Institute of Real Estate Appraisal (AIREA) founded in 1932. The best respected of the professional associations for residential appraisers was the Society of Real Estate Appraisers (SRA). Of course, the AIREA had members who specialized in residential real estate appraisal and the Society had commercial appraisers, and there was substantial overlap in membership. In 1991, after much internal politicking and tearing of hair, the Institute and the Society merged to form (AI) The Appraisal Institute.

The professional associations awarded designations to members who had completed what the organizations believed to be a minimum level of professional education, training and experience, and had demonstrated their ability to prepare a complete appraisal and communicate that appraisal in a narrative report.

The AIREA awarded the MAI designation to commercial appraisers and the RM designation to residential appraisers, and the Society awarded the SRA designation to residential appraisers and the SRPA designation to commercial appraisers. The successor organization, The Appraisal Institute, currently awards only the MAI and the SRA designations to commercial and residential appraisers respectively, although they still recognize the SRPA designated (former) Society members. The Appraisal Institute also established and awards the AI-RRS and AI-GRS designations for residential and general review appraisers.

Earning a designation was, and still is, a first-class pain in the behind. I have worked my way through an MA, an MS and a Graduate Certificate in Real Estate (GCRE), and I believe that earning my MAI designation and, later, my CBA (Certified Business Appraiser) designation from the Institute of Business Appraisers required as much rigorous work as did any of my academic degrees.

Generally speaking, an MAI has to have a college degree [or already be a General Certified Appraiser], pass a series of introductory and advanced courses (now totaling over 400 classroom hours), have 4,500 man-hours of appraisal work reviewed by nationally selected appraisal review screeners, pass a two-day comprehensive exam and prepare a demonstration report that is graded on a national level. The process takes most serious applicants between five and ten years to complete.

The process of becoming designated as an SRA is somewhat less demanding because appraising a one to four family house depends mostly on a comparison of the house to be appraised to other similar or "comparable" houses that recently sold. Residential appraisal usually doesn't depend on an analysis of the economic performance of real estate that is supposed to generate cash flow. Since 2014, earning an SRA requires that an applicant have a four-year degree, pass general and specialized appraisal courses in residential appraisal that total over 195 classroom hours, have 3,000 hours of appraisal work screened, pass a comprehensive exam and prepare a demonstration appraisal or complete a week-long workshop. Anyone who considers the profession seriously should look at the Appraisal Institute's webpage, www.appraisalinstitute.org, for the current requirements and much more useful information.

Following the failure of the savings and loan industry, we appraisers became important enough to be blamed. The Congressional Hearings following the demise of the S&Ls (our big 1989 financial crisis that led to the Resolution Trust Corporation) were titled: "*The Impact of Faulty and Fraudulent Appraisals on the Failure of the Savings and Loan Industry.*" I had barely begun working in the profession and I was already responsible for the failure of an entire component of the economy. The lenders and mortgage brokers (read commissioned salesmen) who had pressured appraisers to meet the home's sales price and who had made the loans had (in the opinion of Congress) nothing to do with the failure of thousands of Savings and Loans institutions. Even following a much bigger crash in 2008, bankers are still not a state- or Federal-regulated profession. One of the likely consequences of this present screw up in mortgage lending may be that the loan officers and mortgage brokers will get to know the joy of being a regulated profession.

In 1989 it was the appraisers' turn to be regulated! FIRREA followed the model for the accounting profession by creating The Appraisal Foundation. The Foundation is made up of two boards, The Appraisal Standards Board, and the Appraisal Qualifications Board. The Appraisal Standards Board (ASB) is responsible for The Uniform Standards of Professional Appraisal Practice (USPAP), which is generally similar to the Financial Accounting Standards Board (FASB). The Appraisal Qualifications Board (AQB) determines the requirements for qualification as an appraiser or as an appraisal school or instructor. In 2010 the Foundation also established the Appraisal Practice Board (APB) to identify and issue guidance on recognized valuation methods and techniques (which may apply to all appraisal disciplines) in the form of Valuation Advisories. This Board utilized panels of Subject Matter Experts (SMEs), which comprise individuals with a range of expertise on the topic being considered. Since the APB Advisories were not rules or regulations that must be followed, the APB was abolished in 2017.

To participate in federally regulated transactions states had to create a method of licensing and regulating appraisers and appraisal instruction in compliance with the AQB and the ASB rules. As mortgages are federally regulated transactions, all states complied to a greater or lesser extent by creating at least two classes of appraisers, Certified Appraisers and Licensed Appraisers. Some states, like Georgia, also require that beginning trainees be approved by the state as "State Registered" or "State Trainee", but trainees may not appraise anything and must work under the direct supervision of a Certified Appraiser.

The beginning level for an actual appraiser is Licensed Appraiser. A Licensed Appraiser may appraise a one to four family house as long as the total value does not exceed $1,000,000. To appraise a shopping center or an apartment house or an office building or almost anything else, one must become a Certified Appraiser. Some states, like Georgia, split the Certified class into a Certified Residential Appraiser, who may appraise any type of residential structure, and a General Certified Appraiser, who may legally appraise anything.

That's me, Georgia General Certified Appraiser No. 202. To put things in perspective, the Appraisal Institute considers a Certified Appraiser as a journeyman appraiser and credits the 300 hours of introductory appraisal education required class work (out of 420 hours) plus the first 3,000 hours of supervised experience (out of the 4,500 hours) as having been accomplished.

Chapter 3: The Expert Witness

Litigation support means that the appraiser is willing to testify. The jury (or in some cases the judge) is the "trier of fact" who in fact determines the value of the property, but the evidence that the judge or jury considers is the appraiser's testimony. Going to court is fearsomely expensive in both money and time, and the outcome is often a crap shoot. There is a lot of truth to the saying: "If you want justice, go to a house of ill repute. If you want to get screwed, go to court!"

As a consequence, most disputes about value settle at some level of negotiation prior to court. The controversies that can't settle usually involve the biggest differences of opinion about value and the more confusing, complicated and unusual properties.

Expert witnesses are permitted in court when the issues require a specialist who has sufficient training and experience to assist the judge and or jury in coming to a reasonable decision. Although the expert witnesses are usually hired by the attorneys and are paid by the litigants, they are independent of any party to the case and their pay cannot be contingent on the outcome of the case.

As a matter of course, I have never been revealed as an expert by an attorney unless he thought that my opinion helped his case, but the only thing that I testify to is my own opinion. I love it when the jury believes me rather than the other guy, but the outcome only impacts my pride, not my paycheck.

Other than my hourly rate, my reward is that I had the chance to solve the appraisal problem and to explain my reasoning through the process of direct testimony and cross-examination. What more could an appraiser desire? As the attorney often gets about a third of a multimillion-dollar award, I would love a piece of the fee, but no one has figured out a way for an expert witness to share in a contingent fee and still avoid any conflict of interest. Consequently, I retired poor and "Denny Crane, Esq." got the scotch and the cigar.

We experts fill an unusual role in the court. Once we are admitted as an expert in the case, we provide opinion evidence. No one else can do this. Most witnesses can only testify to things that they saw or heard or did themselves, and they cannot use what other people tell them (hearsay) to support their testimony. My job is to interview buyers and sellers and brokers and other knowledgeable actors, and then make up my mind about the most probable behavior of the whole marketplace. I ordinarily testify using hearsay evidence.

When I tell the court "facts" about a transaction that I am using as a comparable sale, I only "know" what the buyer or seller or broker tells me about a transaction. In full disclosure states, like Tennessee, the deed recorded at the courthouse includes an affidavit that states the names and contact information for the responsible human (rather than corporate) parties to the sale, the amount of the transaction, the amount financed and other facts that an appraiser finds very useful. In non-disclosure states, like Alabama, the deed says "for $10 and other considerations." Parties to transactions are often Limited Partnerships (LPs) or Limited Liability Companies (LLCs) or other special purpose entities, and the deed tells me very little other than that a transaction took place.

If we, as a society, want more reliability in appraisals and more transparency in the mortgage process, we will require full disclosure for real estate transactions. Very limited disclosure assists criminals involved in mortgage fraud by fooling appraisers into believing that a sale is a legitimate third-party transaction when it really is a flip between related parties.

However, disclosure is gained at the price of privacy. I recall a telephone conversation I had with a doctor in Atlanta who had recently purchased a medical office building. I called him to verify the transaction and I asked him to confirm what I already knew concerning the sales price, the parties to the sale, etc. I still can hear the awful silence on the other end of the phone before he asked how in hell I had so much information about his private business. I explained that it was all in the public record, and he said incredulously, "You mean anyone can learn this?" I guess he had not informed his wife's divorce attorney that he had recently bought the building.

Once I'm "qualified" by the court as an expert in a case, I can testify that the value is $6,350,000, and just shut up and sit down. My opinion about the value of the property in question becomes the evidence that the trier of fact considers. Anything that I say, other than my appraised value, goes to the weight of the evidence. Most of the time, I testify using thousands of words and I am often forced to relearn that "even a bass wouldn't get in much trouble if he learned to keep his big mouth shut!"

Qualifying an expert is done by a process called "voir dire." The attorney who hires you asks questions to bring out your qualifications, and when he sits down, the attorney on the other side does his best to make you look like a fool or a crook. Once he or she sits down, the court decides whether it will admit you as an expert.

Chapter 4: Appraisal Is a Stinking Business

XYZ Grease and Tallow is one of my favorite cases, mostly because of the wonderful characters involved, but also because it revolved around the battle of the appraisers.

XYZ Grease and Tallow was a rendering factory in a rural county. Like most of these places it was well off the beaten path in the county on Snake Creek. The Water Authority condemned the plant in 2001 because it wanted the land as a part of a reservoir. The Special Master awarded $140,000 for the 38 acres of land, and nothing for the plant, the equipment and the business.

A Special Master is a court-appointed "trier of fact," usually an attorney, who is the first hearing officer to determine just and adequate compensation in a condemnation proceeding. The parties to the condemnation can either agree with the Special Master's award, or, without any prejudice, either party has an absolute right to demand a *de novo* trial in Superior Court and the jury will not be informed about the Special Master's earlier decision.

In Georgia there are two instances in which a person can demand a 12-man jury trial. The first, if he or she is on trial for murder; and the second, if the issue involves the value of his real estate. We Georgians have our priorities in the right order.

The owners had paid one of the largest rendering companies in the US $1,000,000 to purchase a plant in 1998 and then invested about another $1,000,000 in 1999 to double the plant's capacity.

A rendering plant is a nasty business. Its function is to turn dead cows, dead horses and grease from restaurant grease traps into two marketable commodities—non-edible meat and non-edible grease. Both are traded daily on the Chicago Mercantile Exchange. The dead animals and restaurant grease become animal feed, lipstick and hundreds of other products most of us don't really want to know too much about. The process whereby this magic transformation takes place is like rendering bacon. Everything is chopped up and cooked. The grease is skimmed off and the "meat" is separated, packaged and shipped. The process stinks like a rancid kitchen at a labor camp, which is why these things are generally not permitted near populated areas.

A rendering plant is mostly a pile of slick physical assets. Most of these assets consist of the land, the buildings, equipment in the plant, the grease traps placed at the restaurants, and specialized trucks used for hauling the grease traps from the restaurants to the plant and others for hauling the "finished goods" away. There is not a lot of intellectual property associated with a rendering plant—no patents or copyright materials, no value to a brand, no highly-skilled workforce.

Restaurants, chicken processing plants, slaughter houses and farmers with dead cows have no legal alternative to dispose of their grease and offal. They must have access to a rendering facility. They can't dump this waste into the sewer or landfill. Consequently, there are contracts between businesses that generate the waste and the rendering plant that make both businesses possible.

Once XYZ was notified by the Water Authority that the plant would be acquired as a part of the reservoir, it had to notify its client restaurants that it could not commit to take their grease. The restaurants found alternative processors. At the actual date of the take, XYZ was closed and out of business.

By selling the trucks, the grease traps and a new centrifuge separator, the owners recouped two hundred thousand dollars of the two-million-dollar investment. They expected to recoup the rest from the condemnation award. Naturally, they believed $140,000 from the Special Master was unjust and inadequate compensation. They hired Bobby Lee Cook and Irwin Stolz as their attorneys. Bobby Lee Cook of Summerville, GA, is one of my state's best-known lawyers. I copied the following opening paragraphs from the March 2009 *American Bar Association Journal*:

The year was 1949. Bobby Lee Cook was handling one of his first-ever murder trials, defending a man who had killed another man who had called him a "goddamn son of a bitch."

During opening statements, the prosecutor told the Dade County, Ga., jurors that while calling someone this was a bad thing, it didn't give the defendant the right to kill the man.

Slowly, Cook rose from his chair at the defense table to approach the jury. "I have a question for you," he asked the dozen in the box. "What would you have done if someone had called you a goddamn son of a bitch?"

At that moment, an older mountain man with a long beard sitting at the back of the jury box whispered just loud enough for the other jurors to hear: "Why, I would have killed the son of a bitch."

"I had an entire opening statement planned," Cook says. "But I just looked at the man, looked at the jurors, nodded, walked back to my chair and sat down."

The next day, the jury acquitted his client.

During the past six decades, Cook has tried thousands of cases, including more than 300 murder trials, in more than 40 states and several countries. He's represented moonshiners and money launderers, bootleggers and bank fraud schemers. The Rockefellers and Carnegies have been his clients. The television show Matlock was reportedly based on Cook's practice. And his defense of Savannah socialite Jim Williams helped bring to life John Berendt's true-crime classic Midnight in the Garden of Good and Evil. At age 82, Cook still lives in Summerville, Ga., which sits a little closer to Chattanooga, Tenn., than to Atlanta. He's still trying cases—he represents three murder defendants in separate cases set to go to trial this year. He remains one of

*the most sought-after criminal defense lawyers in the South.
"I'm having the best and most productive year of my career,"
Cook says. "I enjoy waking up every morning and kicking
somebody in the ass that needs it."*

http://www.abajournal.com/magazine/article/bobby_lee_cook

Irwin Stolz, who is a year younger than Bobby Lee, served on the Georgia Court of Appeals. Before his second retirement he helped form Gambrell & Stolz (now a part of Baker Donelson, one of the country's largest law firms). Judge Stolz currently practices a little law in Athens, Georgia, as a part of Lewis, Stolz, Hurt, Frierson & Grayson, LLP, often serving as second chair on the eminent domain cases he and Bobby Lee are willing to take.

The Georgia Supreme Court had ruled in earlier cases that the market value of property acquired by condemnation under eminent domain was the value of that property *at the date of the condemnation.* However, it had also ruled that a business need not be in business on the date of the take in order to have value.

The Georgia Constitution defines "property" to include intangible property, so in some cases a condemnee can recover the value of the intangible business as well as the value of the tangible real estate and machinery and equipment. As of the actual date of the take, XYZ had been out of business for over a year.

The attorneys instructed me to ignore that inconvenient fact and treat the assignment as if it were an inverse condemnation (which is what happens when a property owner claims that the government has effectively taken his property, even if there has not been a transfer of title via a condemnation).

The attorneys hired a competent machinery and equipment appraiser who was willing to testify that—as of the date that XYZ was forced out of business—the machinery and equipment in place and in service were worth about $1,200,000. As a real estate appraiser, I was willing to testify that the land and buildings in use contributed another $800,000 to the overall value of the enterprise, making up the approximately $2,000,000 that XYZ paid for the facility as expanded.

The real trick, and the essential difference of opinion between me and the opposing appraiser hired by the Water Authority, was that I contended that, as a working plant, XYZ had the capacity to generate enough "profit" or "free net cash flow" to be "worth" $2,000,000. The other guy opined that the plant could not earn enough income to provide an adequate return on the investment.

This is a big point in deciding what something is worth. It may be easy to agree that a pile of assets costs $2,000,000 to assemble. The major flaw in this line of thinking is that things are not necessarily worth what they cost. Any homeowner who has spent $30,000 on a swimming pool will quickly understand this market phenomenon when he learns that the pool only added $10,000 to the house's resale price.

Unless the XYZ Grease and Tallow Company could earn enough money to be worth $2,000,000, it wouldn't matter that the fellows spent $2,000,000 to put it together.

The income approach to appraisal is based on the simple concept that (V) value is equal to (I) income divided by (R) capitalization rate. If one were to believe that the appropriate capitalization rate for the XYZ Grease and Tallow factory was 20%, the income from the plant, after all expenses, would be $400,000—if the plant were to be worth $2,000,000 ($400,000 / .20 = $2,000,000 or five times earnings).

If the stabilized free cash flow was only $300,000, the business would be worth only $1,500,000. If there was nothing left over after paying all bills, the plant would only have been worth salvage value.

Consequently, the argument came down to the appraisers' understanding of the business and the owners' competence to run the business and make money. If you were to look up "good ol' boys" on Wikipedia you would find pictures of the fellows who owned XYZ.

However, either of them could write a cashable check for more than $10,000,000 on their own accounts. One made his fortune turning chicken manure, pine bark and sand into potting soil. The other states proudly that his fortune rests on his ability to haul chicken guts. According to MANTA.com, his trucking company bills between $10 and $20 million dollars per year and employs between 50 and 99 people hauling offal from the chicken processing plants to the rendering plants.

During the four-day trial, the owners, the attorneys and I were holed up in a Columbus, GA, hotel, mostly telling stories. My favorite was one of the fellows' rendition of the time that he and a colleague and their wives were invited to a White House state dinner near the end of the Carter administration. (He never told how much they had contributed to the Carter campaign to get that invitation, but to the best of my memory the story was as follows):

> *"Me and T.... had never been to this fancy a function, and we thought that they had it in for us from the moment we arrived. First, they split us up and we didn't know practically anybody else except Jimmy and Rosalynn, who were sitting so close to me that I had to move my chair whenever Jimmy got up.*
>
> *They sat me with some federal judge named Burger. During dinner he asked me what I did for a living and I told him I hauled chicken guts. That put the quietus to the conversation for a while, but near the end of the dinner he said, "No, I really want to know why you are here." I told him that feller (pointing to Jimmy) knows I am in the trucking business. He has raised the price of fuel from $0.50/gallon to over $2.00/gallon and he raised the cost of interest on the loans I need to buy my trucks to over 20%. He believed I needed one more good dinner before he leaves town!"*

The business appraiser hired by the Water Authority was not impressed with the owners' credentials as businessmen. On cross-examination, when asked why two businessmen would pay $2,000,000 for a plant that was (in his opinion) worth only $140,000, he said that he thought they just didn't know any better.

To clarify this opinion, the opposing appraiser stated that the commodity price of non-edible grease had been steadily drifting downward. Following the mad cow scare the price of non-edible meat had fallen off the table so to speak. By his calculations the price that XYZ could get for its products was below the cost of production. Therefore, the business was worthless.

I said I was impressed with the fact that both the owners had made millions of dollars running successful businesses that were no more complicated than XYZ Grease and Tallow. Also, although I recognized that the commodity price of the end products had fallen below the cost of production, my research into the industry indicated that there was a second factor that must be considered.

The restaurants and the processing plants and the grocery stores and the owners of dead cows and dead horses had no alternative to the rendering plant if their own businesses were to remain open. The rendering plant functioned like the landfill for these businesses. Consequently, when the price of the non-edibles fell, the rendering plants charged to pick up the restaurants' grease and the spoiled meat. The supply and demand for the non-edibles and the limited supply of licensed rendering facilities kept the market in general equilibrium. The cash flow to XYZ and its competitors remained generally constant, regardless of the commodity market price for their end products.

In the real world XYZ Grease and Tallow was worth about $2,000,000 (net of the equipment XYZ had already sold off), which is what the court ruled. The case was appealed to the Georgia Court of Appeals and was upheld.[2]

The appeals court used this case to clarify Georgia law by ruling that when a condemning authority *caused* the closing of a business, it had to pay for the business loss even if the business was not operating as of the date of the taking.

---

[2] 274 Ga. App. 353; decided July 12, 2005.

Chapter 5: More Appraisals of Stinking Businesses

Rendering factories are not the only assignments that helped persuade me that appraisal is a stinking business. I had the pleasure of appraising a sewer plant and a stacked broiler house, both of which are ripe assignments.

A Sewer Plant

The sewer plant was an interesting challenge. This was the type of assignment wherein I was not likely to find three good comparable sales that took place within the last 90 days. This sewer plant became a real-world assignment when a local government decided to condemn a treatment plant. The plant had been built as part of a cotton mill and used to service that industry. The industry changed and no longer needed the treatment facility. A private entrepreneur knowledgeable about the sewer business recognized an opportunity to provide sewer services to the subdivisions that were being constructed in reasonable proximity to the plant. I was hired by an attorney who represented a financial institution that had lent the money for the entrepreneur's acquisition and development.

Life has often been described as a process of water in and water out. People who live in houses in much of America must have a legally approved method of handling their effluent. Most rural and suburban subdivisions handle their wastes using septic tanks, which require drainage fields and "perk" tests. A developer with access to a public sewer system can get double or triple the production of single family lots per acre of land as compared to a subdivision that depends on septic tanks.

The sewer plant in question was constructed circa 1978. According to records at the Environmental Protection Division (EPD) and our interviews with the plant engineer, the treatment plant was designed as a 500,000 gpd (gallons per day) secondary treatment plant. The EPD engineer reported that a 2-mgd (million gallons per day) plant was feasible. A 5-mgd plant would be possible, assuming the sale of gray water and tertiary treatment for some of the effluent.

The entrepreneur owned a company in the business of designing, building and operating private wastewater treatment plants. It is an outgrowth of a company that has been designing wastewater treatment plants in Georgia since 1905. In our opinion the entrepreneur had the ability to own, manage and develop the subject to its full economic potential.

As a practical matter the critical variable required to permit a wastewater treatment plant is the discharge permit. When one entity obtains that permit, it establishes a monopoly position for that river. The permit alone may have substantial value. As long as the plant complies with the state requirements, the sewer plant has effectively established an exclusive right to provide wastewater treatment services to the surrounding area.

The economic value of the sewer plant depends on three features. One feature is the potential capacity of the river to accept treated sewage. A second is the capital cost of improving and operating the plant to treat sewage to the extent that the effluent does not exceed the limits established by the EPD. The third is that there is demand for sewage treatment within a reasonable market area.

We believed that the residential and commercial growth of the area would support a 5-mgd plant, but that it would take between 15 and 20 years to fully absorb 5-mgd capacity. We thought that a plant of this size was technologically possible and economically feasible. We assigned an 80% probability that a 5-mgd plant is the most economically feasible alternative. We assigned a 20% probability that a 2-mgd plant is the most economically feasible alternative.

Because sewer plants are such capital-intensive investments and because discharge permits establish virtual monopolies within the drainage basin that they serve, most sewer plants are municipal utilities. Like the entrepreneur, the County also believed that demand for sewer services would grow in this area and that a wastewater treatment plant would be a profitable venture. They used their power of eminent domain to take the plant and paid into the court the $1,300,000 that the entrepreneur paid to acquire the plant. Under the rules of eminent domain, once an entity that has the power of eminent domain exercises that power, title to the property changes hands, willing seller or not. The following dispute is just about money.

Unfortunately for the County's theory of value, things are not always worth what they cost. Just as it is perfectly possible to pay too much for an asset, it is also possible to pay much less than it is worth. To the seller the plant was functionally obsolete and expensive to maintain. The $1,300,000 paid by the entrepreneur was "found money" as far as the industry was concerned. It had nothing to do with the value of the plant.

We looked at the earnings potential for the sewer plant based on the letters of commitment from nearby developers, estimated the costs to expand the existing plant and construct the required trunk lines, estimated the magnitude and timing of the expected cash flows and the appropriate risks associated with running a sewer plant and estimated the market value at the date of the condemnation was slightly over $6,000,000, more than four times the County's payment into the court.

It just so happened that at the time of the sewer plant condemnation, I was working for the County's eminent domain litigator on another case wherein the condemning authority was the Georgia D.O.T. and that same attorney was representing a condemnee. The G.D.O.T. had taken most of his (and my) client's road frontage along a county road at an intersection with an interstate highway. Although our client was using the property as a storage and truck transfer facility for their multistate furniture business, the highest and best use of the tract was as the site for a hotel and restaurant and/or for a major truck stop. Before the take, the land was worth a great deal of money, and our client was in the process of disposing of the site and placing their transfer facility on a less expensive site.

The impact of the D.O.T.'s road project was to limit access to our client's site to less than 30 feet (too small for a commercial driveway) and to increase the grade difference between the road and the majority of our client's site by about 12 feet. Consequently, the remainder of our client's site was substantially reduced in value. I appraised the damage at more than $2,000,000.

The lawyer who had retained me, our client's real estate expert, the D.O.T.'s land acquisition specialist and I met on the site to discuss the D.O.T.'s offer to purchase the property in lieu of condemnation. I made a great show of presenting our case for the damages, including spotting the place that we could build a periscope so that a truck trying to exit our site could see oncoming traffic before making a running start to the proposed new elevation of the road. G.D.O.T. offered a nice settlement and the lawyer who had retained me was very pleased with me.

What he said was something like: "Hank, you did a great job today and I am glad you were on our side. However, tomorrow when we try the Sewer Case, I'm going to do my best to make you look like the least competent appraiser in Georgia." That is just the nature of the business.

As I was strapping on my armor in preparation for the Sewer Plant hearing I was shocked to get a phone call from the attorney for the finance company (my retaining attorney) telling me that they had settled for approximately $2.7 million. I understood why the finance company had settled. They had been paid what they were owed plus attorney (and expert) fees. I didn't have any idea why the entrepreneur would settle. He was the one who was out the approximately $3 to $4 million in profit to which I was willing to testify.

I was less shocked when I learned that the entrepreneur had just been indicted by the U.S. Department of Justice for bid rigging on other water and sewer projects. Even if he was an innocent victim of arbitrary County action and was going to lose a fortune to which he was entitled in this case, he knew that a jury was not likely to look favorably on a fellow once he has been indicted by the Feds in a criminal case. Juries treat plaintiffs like they do expert witnesses. They have to like you before they will rule in your favor.

A Double-Stacked Broiler House

I like chickens. Generally, I like them roasted, but a broiled chicken is also welcome at my table. Like most of us I thought that chickens came gutted, plucked and wrapped in plastic, just as I find them in the grocery store. Imagine my surprise when an estate I was appraising included a double-stacked broiler house on a farm about 40 miles outside of the city. The building was a long structure built against the side of a hill. One drive led to a doorway on the top of the hill, and another drive led to large double doors on the lower level.

Good fortune favored me as we drove up, because the farmer was waiting at the doorway on the top of the hill. We walked into a building as long as a football field filled with stacked cages, each holding a growing chicken. Growing chickens are machines to transform corn into chicken and fertilizer. Gravity carried the corn to the chickens and the fertilizer from the chickens to the lower level of the structure. The field inspection was a less than fragrant experience, but much better than it would have been had the farmer not been standing at the doors on the upper level. I learned a lifelong lesson on that assignment. If you are to inspect a double-stacked broiler house, don't go in the downstairs doors!

Chapter 6: Litigation Support

Juries are very strange decision-making bodies. A dozen strangers from all walks of life are thrown together to sit and listen to hours of arguments by professional arguers. They seldom can ask any questions for themselves. Finally, after the lawyers are finished and the judge issues arcane instructions, the jurors are locked in a room and expected to come to a group decision.

One of the best educational experiences I ever had was serving as a jury foreman for a murder trial. During four days of testimony I thought I was with a reasonable group of people who were learning the same facts I was learning. When the bailiff locked the door my fellow jurors turned into the biggest bunch of damn fools I have ever met! It was hard to believe that we had all been at the same trial. Three days later we still had a hung jury. This was in a trial wherein the accused admitted in court that he shot the guy five times.

I've learned over the years that as a witness you will have about two minutes of the jury's attention. They will listen to your qualifications during voir dire, but when you start to testify, you only get a minute or two before the jury members' eyes glaze over. The jury isn't really going to listen to and weigh all your cogent arguments. What the jury is really going to decide is whether they like you better than they like the expert on the other side. If they like you, they are more likely to trust you. If they trust you, they will be much more likely to accept your opinion.

Pretesting the Expert and His Opinion

Voir dire is an important part of the show. This is when your attorney gets to brag that you are the best-qualified expert in the trial. I tried to differentiate myself by earning designations, publishing articles, earning advanced academic degrees, teaching and being elected to an office in my professional association. I wanted to get this information before the jury in voir dire.

The qualification process is the first time that the jury sees and hears you and this is the time to make as good an impression as possible. If it is only a bench trial (just a judge, no jury) and you have testified before that judge and opposing counsel before, the attorneys will usually stipulate that you are an expert and you won't get the chance to brag.

However, if you are an old grey hair like me with more initials after your name than in your name, you want to let the jury know that your opinion is based on a lifetime of education, training and experience. In essence, you want to press home the point that you are more believable than the inexperienced kid the opposing counsel hired.

Up until 1993 the courts allowed anyone who had been qualified as an expert to testify to an opinion—no matter how "inventive" or imaginative. Nowadays, it is no longer sufficient to be qualified as an expert in a case and let the jury decide which expert to believe.

Court is probably the origin of the expression: "If you can't dazzle them with your footwork, baffle them with your bullshit!" However, in an attempt to reduce the influence of unfounded BS, the U.S. Supreme Court in the 1993 Daubert case and the 1999 Kuhmo Tire case, ruled that an expert could only testify to an opinion that was formed using the recognized body of knowledge in that field.

If there is doubt about the appraiser's methodology, the court holds a separate "Daubert" hearing (not in the presence of the jury) to determine whether the jury will be permitted to hear the expert's evidence. This is the court's attempt to prevent the jury from being influenced by junk science. Professional meetings, journals and books— not the courts—are the correct forum to expand the body of knowledge.

The Independent Man

An appraiser is, by definition, unbiased, even though he is hired by one of the parties to the suit. I try hard to protect my independence by being paid before I show up in the court house. I love going to court, but only when I can charge for the privilege. I am not excited about going into court as a plaintiff, especially to try to sue a law firm for a fee. I try to always bill against a retainer so that I can tell the court that I have no skin in the game. I was only stiffed for a fee three times in a 35-year career. Most recently, I wound up at the back of a long line of creditors in a bankruptcy case. I'm indeed lucky that this client only refused to pay the fee. In the summer of 2009 he was arrested for murdering his wife.

Another great protection to my independence is to arrange to be fired and to be able and willing to fire my client. My best tool has been to have a written "Agreement for Appraisal Services" in two parts to protect the attorney and his client from unwarranted discovery and to have a retainer on which I draw for my hourly charges.

In the first phase of the assignment I act as a valuation consultant to the attorney. As a consultant all my work and my oral report to the attorney are protected by the court as "attorney work product" and can't be discovered by opposing counsel. I try to arrange to be paid a retainer for this work before the client knows what my opinion will be. If the client lies to me too much or fails to provide me the operating history for the asset to be appraised, I fire the client and deduct the earned fee from the retainer.

Once the attorney knows what I am willing to testify to, he can fire me if my opinions don't help his case. His other option is to accept my opinions and reveal me to the other side as his expert. At this point I am paid to prepare my affidavit or memorandum for testimony or appraisal report in the format the retaining attorney prefers.

It is a violation of the Appraisal Institute Code of Ethics for a member to provide any testimony without having first prepared a written file memorandum. The Uniform Standards of Professional Appraisal Practice (USPAP) are not as clear as the Institute on this point, but I was told by a Georgia Real Estate Appraisal Board staff inspector that the Board believes that an appraiser who testified without having prepared a written memorandum or having a complete written file would be in violation of USPAP. I must keep my state license if I am going to pursue my profession, so if the Georgia Board's staff wants me to have a written file or memorandum before testimony, I will have one.

In most Federal courts under the Federal Rules of Civil Procedure my report takes the place of my direct testimony, and I will only be subject to cross-examination. In Federal court the words in the appraisal report really count.

Once I am revealed as an expert, opposing counsel is entitled to almost everything in my file, including e-mails, spreadsheets and other electronic files. I save almost everything, because the retaining attorney can identify some things in my file as "attorney work product" and refuse to give them to the other side. However, I keep only the most recent version of my report. I don't want multiple versions available to anyone. All work on the report, up to the final version, carries a "DRAFT" watermark on each page and/or a heading that reads "Incomplete Report, Attorney Work Product." Opposing counsel's job is to impeach my credibility. There is no sense in handing him or her an earlier version of my own work wherein I might impeach myself.

I can't make the call about what from my file I wish to show opposing counsel. If I get a *subpoena duces tecum* I must respond by producing everything I have in my files. The translation of the Latin is "bring with you under penalty of punishment," and I do not want to be punished! If there is any question I turn over my complete file to the retaining attorney and he edits the file to protect his privilege. Up to the time the appraiser receives a subpoena, he or she can edit the files, and should keep nothing that the appraiser did not rely upon in making his or her appraisal. It is a little embarrassing to have to read out in open court my e-mail describing the other side's expert as a pushover or that his appraisals are "made as instructed" or anything else I may have thought but shouldn't have said out loud or in writing.

Chapter 7: What Is an Appraisal?

Jim Pritchett had a plaque on his wall that was a quote from some judge saying: *"An appraisal isn't an art and it isn't a science, it's a mystery!"* I wish I had that citation. There was a judge who had it right.

An appraisal is an independent opinion of some stated standard of value, which itself is based on a premise of value, and is made by a qualified appraiser (at least a Licensed or Certified Appraiser if it is real property). The opinion must comply with the recognized body of appraisal knowledge (usually contained within USPAP). The opinion must be credible. The defining criterion for "credibility" is whether appraisal peers would find the opinion worthy of being believed.

An appraisal is made up of two parts. The first part is the process of forming the opinion of value. At this stage of the game the appraiser's primary job is to keep from fooling himself. The second part of the process is to communicate the opinion in such a way that the appraiser does not fool anyone else.

Communication can be oral or in writing. Since most users of appraisal services want some record to cover their assets, most appraisals are committed to writing. Appraisers who are governed by USPAP must have a written appraisal file, even if they only communicate their opinion orally.

Written appraisals can be "form appraisals," which is what you usually see for residential appraisals. Fannie Mae and others, like the Appraisal Institute, developed these forms to be certain that the appraisal covers all the facts that lenders want to be included and that all the same pieces of information are in the same spot on all the forms so that underwriters and reviewers know where to look. In Georgia, and in many other states, the Department of Transportation requires that appraisers working for the D.O.T. right-of-way (ROW) acquisitions use the Department's appraisal forms for the same reasons.

Commercial appraisers sometimes use approved form reports for less complicated properties or in circumstances wherein the client requires a form, but most use a written narrative report of lesser or greater detail. The simplest can be a letter that states the critical appraisal judgments, which include:

- the interest in the property being appraised,
- the standard of value applied,
- the judgment of the property's highest and best use,
- the basic facts upon which the appraisal judgment is based,
- the generally recognized appraisal approaches and methodologies, and
- the appraiser's opinion of value.

These days most clients require a summary appraisal report wherein the appraiser summarizes the reasoning and the judgments listed above or she could prepare a detailed report that constitutes the 80 to 200-page file stuffers that have been the MAI's stock in trade.

Appraisers are legally obligated only to their clients, but appraisal reports have a life of their own and are out of the appraiser's control. To make this point clear most careful appraisers include a "shrink wrap" clause in each report. This is a statement that specifies the intended user and the intended use of the appraisal. It states that anyone other than the intended user who reads the appraisal report agrees that they are on their own. The appraiser is not liable for any action that the "non-intended" user may or may not take based on the appraiser's opinion. This provision is similar to the software industry's statement that anyone who opens the shrink wrap on a software CD agrees to the terms and conditions of the company's contract with its users.

The appraiser still has an obligation not to mislead the reader. How much information should an appraiser put into a description of a region or of a neighborhood? If I know that I am writing for a Buckhead, Atlanta lender about a Buckhead property, I am wasting everyone's time and money if I write three pages that describe the foundation of Atlanta as "Marthasville" based on the name of some railroad engineer's child or that Sherman burned the place to the ground. On the other hand, if the report is going to a California lender, I probably should write enough to let the reader know what is happening to the local economy of this section of Atlanta, and why I think that the subject property will or will not be economically successful in this micro-location.

Always, whatever the appraisal report format, the appraiser's goal is to communicate the "who, what, where, when and why" of his opinion in such a way that he intends to lead the reader to the same conclusion that the appraiser reached when he was asking himself "what is this thing worth?" I am still reminded of the utility of my freshman English professor, John Shaw's, advice that I should write as if I was designing a bikini. I must write enough to cover the essentials, but keep it brief enough to make it interesting.

Chapter 8: Up to Our Ass in Alligators; Appraising the Everglades

Sometime in 1997 Jim got a call from an old colleague, Jim Eaton, who was the chief appraiser for the U.S. Department of Justice. The government wanted to acquire all the land south of Alligator Alley (I-75 crossing Florida from the east coast to the west coast) plus a little on the east side of Florida near Miami to expand the Everglades National Park and the Big Cypress Preserve and to permit the Corps of Engineers to redo some of the plumbing that makes up the L-31 Canal. For almost 100 years the Corps had been draining the swamp to assist big agriculture in growing more sugarcane and West Palm, Fort Lauderdale, Miami and dozens of little Florida cities in growing more people.

The freshwater wetlands of south Florida form one of the most unusual ecosystems in the world. The land slopes downward from Lake Okeechobee southward to Key West at a grade change of about one foot per mile. It rains a lot in Florida, and there is a slow sheet flow of water southward making up the largest swamp in the country. Most of the good citizens of Miami, and almost all the ones we aren't too proud of, live on land made from draining the swamp. All 10,000,000 of them drink the water that percolates through the vegetation and muck and limestone to recharge the aquifer.

All our "improvements" in the south Florida wetlands and all the freshwater drawn from the aquifer have led to salt water infiltration into the aquifer endangering the potable water supply. At the same time fertilizer in the runoff from the sugar plantations has led to a choking algae growth that has seriously degraded the ecology of the Everglades and the Big Cypress.

In 1989 Congress passed a law to acquire about 600,000 acres that it did not already own south of Alligator Alley. About 10,000 separate private owners owned this land and the government forecast that about 20% or 2,000 would not want to sell and their land would have to be acquired by condemnation. The Environment and National Resources Division (ENRD) of the US Department of Justice handles cases wherein an agency of the US government condemns private property. The law set up a Commission to try these cases.

Whenever any government acquires private property by condemnation, the Constitution requires that they pay "just and adequate compensation." Just and adequate compensation begins with the market value of the part to be taken by the government, but how do you know what that means?

Any of us who owns property and wants to sell has an opinion of how much we think our property is worth. We expose the property to the market for a little more than we hope to get to give ourselves a little bargaining room. If we have been realistic in our expectations, we have a reasonable chance that someone out there in the marketplace will offer a price close enough to what we think fair to make a transaction possible.

In eminent domain condemnation proceedings, by definition, the owner does not want to sell. The law states that the only person who can testify to a judgment about market value, other than the owner, is an appraiser. Consequently, the government hires an appraiser to determine "market value." If the property owner disagrees with the government's opinion, he hires his own appraiser and some neutral court "tries the case," which is really a battle of the appraisers. Society has generally agreed that this system is fairer than trial by combat or other systems of justice that have even greater pitfalls than our adversarial judicial system.

The Everglades and the Big Cypress are pretty much undifferentiated lands. As any of you who have looked out of an airplane window when you are over the southern part of Florida can attest, one or two photographs will show you the whole thing. There is a "sea of grass" spotted with "hammocks" or circles of trees. Most of the land is underwater between three months and nine months of the year, and the water ranges from a few inches deep to a few feet deep, except for the rivers and channels or man-made canals.

The western side of the state, or the Big Cypress Preserve area, used to have more trees than the Everglades, but the Collier Company and others logged out most of the Cypress decades ago.

The sheet flow and overall ecology is slightly different on the west side of Florida, but not so much that most of us would notice. There are very few places within this area where people live, and there is very little agriculture other than at the borderlands. The "highest and best use" of most of the lands is to flow and percolate water and support the flora and fauna that nature intended (plus others, like the para grass, the Brazilian peppertree, anacondas and boa constrictors that nature may not have intended in the South Florida wetlands). Most of the rational legal use of this land by man is for hunting and fishing.

When faced with an undeveloped tract of land, about the only evidence of value upon which an appraiser can rely is the sale of generally similar undeveloped tracts of land (the sales comparison approach to value). When there is not much to differentiate one parcel from another parcel it becomes much more difficult for an appraiser to understand why one 100-acre parcel sold for $500/acre and another very similar 100-acre parcel sold for $5,000/acre.

An appraiser's basic working hypothesis is that a rational, economically motivated man tries to maximize his financial return and minimize his financial costs. When two such motivated rational people acting without any duress and with generally the same access to information transfer title to property for cash, the transaction is an indication of the behavior of a rational marketplace.

I know that this "rational, economically motivated man" rubric asks a great suspension of disbelief, but it is the model upon which we have settled because we couldn't think of anything else that seems more reasonable. Consequently, an appraiser examines the property to be appraised to try to distinguish competitive differentials that may be recognized by the marketplace. Some of these may be size of the tract, view, proximity to a paved road, trees and ponds, etc. She then compares the competitive differentials on parcels that in fact sold in a free and open marketplace to the characteristics of the "subject" property to make a judgment about the price that the market would pay for the subject as of the effective date of the appraisal.

The rules of our game require that we consider at least three real-world "comparable" transactions before we make our judgment. Three is the minimum because three observations are the fewest number that one can consider to reach any measure of both the dispersion of the data and the central tendency of the data.

If you find three similar properties that sold at about the same time as your effective appraisal date at $4,750/acre, $5,000/acre and $5,250/acre, you could feel pretty good about saying that the market value of the subject of your appraisal is about $5,000/acre. On the other hand, if one tract sold at $2,500/acre, another sold at $5,000/acre and a third sold at $7,500/acre, the average value would still be $5,000/acre, but you would probably like to look for a fourth or fifth "comparable" sale before you made a judgment about the market value of the subject. The fourth and fifth comparable sale might indicate that $7,000/acre to $7,500/acre was the more likely market value, and that the $2,500/acre sale and the $5,000/acre sale were aberrations.

The Justice Department was faced with the task of hiring dozens of appraisers who would have to function as expert witnesses on hundreds of condemnation cases. The evidence in each case would be the appraisal of a specific tract of land in the swamp as of the date of the condemnation.

The Environmental and Natural Resource Division of the Justice Department (ENRD) lawyers knew that transaction prices of specific parcels in the swamp varied all over the place. It would be possible to find three actual sales that "proved" that the market value of a specific tract was $7,500/acre and to have three similar sales that "proved" that the market value of the subject was $500/acre if all that one looked at were three or four actual transactions.

Over a 25-year horizon the National Parks Department, the Corps of Engineers, the Department of the Interior, the South Florida Water Management Division and the State of Florida had commissioned hundreds of appraisals of the south Florida freshwater wetlands. In these appraisals competent appraisers had reported on thousands of actual transactions as evidence for their value opinions. All this data was preserved within their appraisal reports, and these agencies had copies of 25 years of appraisals.

My firm, Pritchett, Ball & Wise, Inc., was hired by the Justice Department to examine these thousands of transaction records to see whether we could identify the variables that in fact affected the market value of this type of land. The study we prepared was released on the web under the Freedom of Information Act, and you can read the report if you go to http://www.justice.gov/enrd/East_Everglades_Report.html or Google "Henry J. Wise" and "Everglades." Even though we published this report in March of 1999, I was asked to prepare to testify on this work as recently as November 2009. Cases have a life of their own, which makes retiring from the expert witness part of the appraisal business somewhat of a chancy thing.

Perhaps the most interesting thing that I learned during the research for this report was the existence of Looneyville. I thought it an apt description of a town for anyone who wished to live there, but it seems that in the 1930s a man named Looney acquired a section of land from the Collier Company and sold off 10 to 200-acre parcels to folks who did not want neighbors. This place was about two hours' drive from the nearest bottle of milk. To get there one drove along Alligator Alley to a place where it crossed an old Collier Company canal, made a 90-degree turn down the embankment of the Expressway, drove along a gravel road made from the spoils of digging the canal, crossed an old iron bridge and entered what was home for about 250 families.

Some folks lived in lean-to shacks usually used for weekend fish camps, and others had 3,000 square foot (sf) ranch houses adjacent to a private airstrip. For a while there were lots of funny- smelling cigarettes coming out of Looneyville, and the US BATF and DEA had a lot of interest in the area. During a field trip to inspect and verify a transaction, Jim Pritchett and I visited a family living in a nice cypress home built on stilts. There were about three generations of the family sitting on the long staircase leading out of the swamp. I don't think I counted more than four teeth amongst the lot of them.

The Feds acquired all of Looneyville as a part of the expansion project. In writing this section I Googled "Looneyville" and found the following on the web.[3] I don't know who the author is, but I give full attribution to his comments. I only wish I could write as well:

> *Looneyville, FL. It's an abandoned town out in the everglades (supposed to be abandoned), I don't know what it used to be called but I've only heard it referred to as Looneyville. I went with a few friends and its creepy as ****. It looks like everyone just all of the sudden dropped what they were doing and left. Kinda like they still live their(sic) but everything is rusty and broke down. We went through a burned down house and heard some really strange noises so we ran outside only to be attacked by an emu. We had to hop a fence to get away from that, then as we were taking a break we heard a chainsaw fire up so we ran like crazy. Never been back, might go if someone has a gun or something (just to be safe, lol).*

What Do You Do When There Is Too Much Data?

When we began this assignment, we were told that we had to look at about 100 sales. The data arrived in six big boxes and turned out to be about 2,500 sales. Many times, different appraisers had used the same sales in different assignments and each sale's write-up (describing the motivations of the buyer and the seller, the terms of the transactions,

---

[3] I found this webpage in 2009 when I began writing, but in 2017 I had no luck in trying to relocate the original source of the quote at http://www.mlgpro.com/forum/showthread. php?t=240371&page=4. However, I found several current references to Looneyville, Florida.

and anything else the appraiser thought useful) was usually different.

Intuitively we are all usually considering data in two categories, either as causes or as outcomes. As we consider the stock market we say that an improved earnings outlook "caused" the price per share to increase or that the larger the house the higher the price. The "causative" variable we consider to be a competitive differential or an independent variable and the outcome, price per acre for example, is the dependent variable. We believe that changes in the independent variables "cause" changes in the dependent variables.

We entered all the data into a Microsoft Access database and combined all the information we had about each sale into a single record for each sale. We eliminated any sale that obviously didn't meet the definition of a market-based transaction (sales from fathers to children or sales in lieu of foreclosure, etc.). We re-verified the data with either the broker, buyer or seller. After all this work we wound up with 785 individual sales that we believed would stand up to court scrutiny. It turned out that 392 of these sales were in the Big Cypress part of the swamp, and 393 were in the East Everglades. Because the average price per acre and the standard deviation of the East Everglades sales were significantly different from the Big Cypress sales, we split the database into two and conducted two different studies.

In a sales comparison approach to the valuation of property the appraiser tries to identify the competitive differentials that the market finds to be important, such as size of property or proximity to a paved road. As we had so many sales, so much data, we knew that we would need a more powerful analytical tool than just looking. We had determined to use a stepwise multilinear regression model. To do this all the data had to be represented by a cardinal number (a number that meant something, rather than just a label). Dollars, as well as size in acres, are cardinal numbers. These can be added, subtracted, multiplied and divided. However, some useful competitive differentials, such as proximity to a paved road, are labels. To turn these labels into something that the statistical program could use, we had to introduce unique dummy variables which were a 1 or a 0. That meant if we had a sale of a 5-acre tract on a paved road we needed a column (independent variable) for that sale entering a 1 in the column if it were on a paved road and a 0 if it wasn't. The same was true for a 5 to 10-acre tract or a 10 to 20-acre tract or a 30 to 50-acre tract or a 50 to 100-acre tract or a 100 to 200-acre tract, etc. You can see that the number of independent variables that had to be considered grew in a hurry. By the time we had finished parsing the data, we had a spreadsheet with 181 columns of independent variables and 392 or 393 rows of sales. Most of the cells were 1s or 0s. We used $/acre for the land as the dependent variable.

We finished our analysis and notified the Justice Department attorneys that we had identified 11 variables that affected the value of land in the Everglades and 10 variables that affected the value of land in the Big Cypress. Once we knew what they were they all made sense. For example, there are only four bridges across the L-31N Canal, which separates the developed eastern side (Fort Lauderdale through Miami) from the Everglades. Unless the property was "near" (within one mile) of one of these bridges the value was lower, all other variables held constant, because a person had to drive a long way to one of these bridges and then drive a long way down the canal spoils road to get to one's property. We scheduled a meeting and the ENRD attorneys gathered in our conference room and we presented our findings.

Dave Vollenweider, Esq., listened to our explanation that we had run an SPSS at the 0.05 level of rejection. Dave listened patiently and asked, "How do you know?"

I started over, more slowly this time, to explain that we had used a stepwise multilinear regression model using the Statistical Package for Social Science (SPSS) wherein we tested all 181 independent (potential causative) variables each in combination with every other independent variable in all possible combinations. We considered a variable to be a possible causative variable if there was a 90% greater than chance probability that it had an impact on $/acre and kept the variable if it maintained a 95% greater than chance probability of having had an impact on $/acre. Dave again asked, "How do you know?"

I spent the next month or more and about 20 pages of the report trying to explain basic descriptive and inferential statistics in as simple words as I could. It took me years to realize that Dave was probably a better statistician than I was. It wasn't that he didn't understand the analytical tool I was using. He wanted to be certain that I could persuade a layman member of a jury that my analysis was reasonable and that I understood what I was doing. Below I have quoted a couple of paragraphs from the Report on the East Everglades[4]:

The mean and standard deviation are also the most useful descriptive statistics because they are mathematical constructs, which means that they can be measured and compared mathematically. This ability is particularly helpful with data, such as that generated by the subject, where "answers" are not readily apparent.

EXAMPLE OF MEAN AND STANDARD DEVIATION FROM TWO DATA ARRAYS

SALE NO.	MARKET A; $/ACRE	MARKET B $/ACRE
1	$7,250	$5,250
2	$6,450	$4,950
3	$6,150	$5,150
4	$5,350	$7,250
5	$5,500	$4,750
6	$5,000	$5,000
7	$4,200	$5,050
8	$4,200	$2,500
9	$3,400	$5,150
10	$2,500	$4,950
MEAN	$5,000	$5,000
STANDARD DEVIATION	$1,377	$1,072

[4] MARKET STUDY; EAST EVERGLADES REPORT, FIRST REVISION, p. 13 of 87.

For example, if we partition or split the array of data into two sets based on some observed difference, such as date-of-sale in the hypothetical example above, we may find that both sets have the same average price per acre (a mean of $5,000/acre), but that the standard deviation of one set (Market B) is substantially smaller than the standard deviation of the other set (Market A). A comparison of the two average values alone may lead to an erroneous judgment that the observed difference in market areas doesn't matter, whereas a comparison of the two standard deviations shows that difference in market area probably does affect the price per acre.

A mathematically based, statistical analysis could make use of the difference in the standard deviation of the two arrays to assign a probability that any observed relationship (average value given market area in this example) was just due to chance for Market A, but that it was statistically significant (probably not due to chance given a stated confidence interval) for Market B. If all we know about the two groups of sales is the sales price/acre, the only statistics we can use to "best" describe the data are statistics about central tendency (like the average, the median and the mode(s)) and statistics about dispersion (like the standard deviation and the range).

Chapter 9: Demystifying the Appraisal Report

It Is All in What You Call It

Rumpole of the Bailey, John Mortimer's beloved character, once explained that his job as a barrister was not much different from that of a taxi driver. He claimed that he had no control over who hailed his cab. His job was to represent whoever hired him to the best of his ability. That is how I feel about my job as an appraiser. Real people have real problems that require my services. I didn't care what it was that was to be valued. I just tried my best to estimate the value.

There are several "Standards of Value" that may be appropriate. The most usual is *market value.* Market value is defined by the Standards of all the appraisal associations that subscribe to USPAP and by most courts as:

> *The most probable price which a property should bring in a competitive and open market under all conditions requisite to a fair sale, the buyer and seller each acting prudently and knowledgeably, and assuming the price is not affected by undue stimulus. Implicit in this definition is the consummation of a sale as of a specified date and the passing of title from seller to buyer under conditions whereby:*
>
> 1. *Buyer and seller are typically motivated;*
> 2. *Both parties are well informed or well advised, and acting in what they consider their own best interests;*
> 3. *A reasonable time is allowed for exposure in the open market;*

4. *Payment is made in terms of cash in U.S. dollars or in terms of financial arrangements comparable thereto; and,*

5. *The price represents the normal consideration for the property unaffected by special or creative financing or sales concessions granted by anyone associated with the sale.*

(12 C.F.R. Part 34.42(g); 55 Federal Register 34696, August 24, 1990, as amended at 57 Federal Register 12202, April 9, 1992; 59 Federal Register 29499, June 7, 1994.)

Market value is a convenient fiction, or, perhaps, a convenient fantasy. It doesn't represent any actual transaction in the marketplace. If an actual seller and buyer were to act prudently and knowledgeably and neither was under any duress, the best way to describe that transaction is as an *investment value.* That is the value of any asset to any specific investor. Only when one looks at a large number of "investment value" transactions does one have a chance at finding market value.

Looking at a "large number" of actual transactions is the secret both to the reliability of an appraisal and to the cost of an appraisal. No one is willing to pay me thousands of dollars to tell them the market value of one share of stock in the Coca-Cola Company. Thousands of entirely fungible shares are sold every day and the statistics are reported for free, or almost for free, in the pages of the financial press or on the internet.

However, the interests in real estate and businesses that I appraise are not fungible. Even two cookie cutter houses in a tract subdivision have some differences. One may be on a corner and another is in the middle of a block or on a cul-de-sac. One may have a backyard pool, and the other may have a wine cellar in the basement. No two franchise fast food restaurants in effect operate in the same marketplace. They may be generally similar enough to be considered reasonable substitutes for each other, but they are not truly fungible, and the appraiser has to make judgments about how the market has priced these differences.

The second part of the problem is that there really are not that many transactions that may reasonably be considered functional equivalents. The more unusual the asset, the fewer actual transactions are available to be considered as indications of market value. I've appraised several tourist attraction caves. I could never find three sales of show caves that took place in the neighborhood over the past three months.

This stuff isn't rocket science. Every appraisal report contains the seeds of its own success or destruction. All it takes is reading the words with a critical and skeptical mind. Unfortunately, most folks who read an appraisal report are lenders who have a vested interest in getting to a specific number that they knew before they hired the appraiser. Until something goes terribly wrong real people do not go through the boring process of reading anything more than the appraiser's letter of transmittal or a single-page summary.

Pretend for a moment that you in fact must critically read an appraisal report. The first thing to look for is a clear description of the subject of the appraisal. It may be that the appraisal is of the whole (fee simple) interest in a specific real property. That is the simplest example, because the premise behind the estimate of value is that the title to the property was transferred for cash as of a specific date between two willing parties, each acting in his own best economic interest. The premise also assumes that neither party was under any duress, and that the property had been on the open marketplace for a sufficient period of time to be exposed to the universe of potential buyers likely to be interested in that specific property.

Much of the time the subject of the appraisal is something less than the whole megillah. If the property to be appraised is leased, the value ought to reflect the terms and conditions of the leases and the appropriate description is an appraisal of the leased fee interest.

If the lease reflects market conditions as of the effective date of the appraisal, there is generally no difference between the market value of the leased fee interest and the market value of the fee simple interest. However, if the property is under a long-term lease at $4.00/sf and today one could easily rent the property for $10.00/sf, there is a big difference between the value of the leased fee interest and the fee simple interest. Consequently, the reader must know what is in fact to be appraised.

Discounts Count

Any asset being appraised is measured against other reasonably similar assets. The house you are considering buying or selling is measured against generally similar houses that have recently sold. The value of the most likely future stream of income from the apartment house you are considering buying is measured against the stream of income from similar apartment houses that recently sold. The value of a share of stock or a bond in a privately held company is measured against stock in similar privately held companies that actually sold and against generally similar publicly traded stocks and bonds.

If you are buying a whole company, the value estimate reflects the fact that you will have control of the company you are buying, and you can make the changes that you think you should make and you can sell that whole company whenever you think the time is ripe.

The issue is even more complicated than my simple illustrations imply. Your decision to buy a house is complicated by the possibility that you might rent a house or an apartment and preserve your mobility and your capital. When a potential investor considers buying real estate he must also consider the advisability of spending that same pool of capital to buy publicly traded stocks or bonds or an interest in a private company. All these possible investments are in competition with each other.

On the other hand, if you are gifting your children 30% of the shares in Wise & Associates, Inc., a privately owned consulting company, your kids will not have any control over the direction or management of Wise Ass. Inc. If the company made $100,000 in profits, as minority shareholders the kids wouldn't have any right to $30,000 in distributions. Unless I decided to pay dividends, the kids may not realize any economic benefit from their stock. If they complained, they would be lucky to get their allowances! This is the problem faced by a minority owner who has no control of any privately held asset.

The kids face another difficulty. If they attempt to sell their shares, there is no regular marketplace where they can list the shares. They may have to go door-to-door or pay 10% to 50% of the proceeds from the sale to a private placement broker. There is no private company market equivalent to Wall Street. If Wise Ass. Inc. were Accenture or KPMG Consulting, both of which are publicly traded consulting companies, the kids could expect to get somewhere between the high and low bid price on the day they sold and have the cash within three days. The transaction costs would be nominal, as little as $0.50/trade using some internet broker. This is the reference point for the marketability of an asset, a big active market of buyers and sellers, nominal trading costs and cash in three days.

Consequently, if the asset to be appraised is a 30% interest in Wise Ass. Inc., then the reader ought to expect that the market extracts a penalty and recognize that there is a difference between a marketable, publicly held company and Wise Ass. Inc. The reader should also recognize the weakness associated with a minority position's lack of control and lack of marketability.

Real Estate Also Has Marketability and Liquidity Problems

Real estate assets constitute what the economists call a "bulky good." Most improved properties take a relatively long time to build and they last 30 to 50 years or longer. They generally take a long time to sell and the brokerage costs are significant, often between 4% and 10% of the transaction price of the asset.

An appraisal of the market value of the fee simple interest in real estate takes all these factors into account. The real estate appraisal assumes that the property had been exposed to the market for the relatively long period typical for that type of property and in that marketplace as of the effective date of the appraisal. That means if a house typically takes six months to sell and the effective date of the appraisal is July 1, the appraisal assumes that the sellers began marketing that house on or about January 1, about 6 months earlier.

If the transaction price for a comparable sale was $200,000 and the brokerage commission was 6%, the appraiser recognizes that the seller was willing to pay someone $12,000 to sell the house, and he pays attention to the $200,000 that the buyer had to pay, not the $188,000 that the seller got to keep.

Also, as most real estate is financed with a blend of equity and debt (mostly debt), the appraiser doesn't pay any attention to the amount of the mortgage unless the sale was financed by the seller at terms different from those typically available in the marketplace.

"When" Matters

It is very important to pay attention to the effective date of the appraisal. Anyone who has found himself under water on a mortgage can attest that property values indeed do change over time, and that the change is not always up. We recently had to make an appraisal of a 50% limited partnership interest in a family limited partnership (FLP) as of two different dates about six months apart. The partnership's assets were a pool of real estate assets. There were no changes in the actual assets that made up the pool, but the value of the pool dropped by about 20% between June of 2008 and January of 2009.

It took about six months before the magnitude of the real estate collapse was recognized by the marketplace, but with real estate six months is a very short time. Recognizing that the marketplace extracts discounts for lack of control and discounts for lack of marketability, it is reasonable to expect that a 50% limited partnership interest in an FLP is going to be worth a lot less than 50% of the pool of real estate assets owned by the partnership, even if the value of the pro rata share of the underlying assets is the beginning point.

The June appraisal was to accompany a tax return for a gift made to the grantor's children. The January appraisal was to accompany an estate tax return reflecting the grantor's date of death. Both appraisals were to be sent to the IRS and probably would be reviewed by the same IRS officer. A share or "unit" in an FLP is an intangible, just as a share of stock is an intangible.

Between June and January, the stock market lost about 40% of its value, reflecting a very different marketplace for all intangible assets. The net effect of a 20% decrease in the market value of the underlying real estate plus a big decrease in the value of intangibles as a class of assets meant that our appraisal of the 50% FLP in January 2009 was a hell of a lot lower than the appraisal of the same assets in June 2008.

The IRS hates discounts of any kind. Over the years they have reluctantly accepted discounts for lack of control and lack of marketability for minority shares in privately held companies and for LLCs, LLPs, FLPs and the other "pass-through" entities that have been created to make wealth disappear from the grasp of the tax man. However, the IRS has consistently lost tax court case after tax court case wherein it tries to limit discounts.

The IRS regulations state that when valuing minority interests the burden of proof of the amount of the discount (from the proportional share of the underlying asset) is on the taxpayer, and the only effective evidence of a discount is the testimony of a competent appraiser (See *Tax Coordinator*, p-6150,6151). Isn't this an amazing profession? The law requires that folks employ me.

However, tax attorneys and tax advisors and taxpayers don't like pulling on the dragon's tail, and our client, the tax attorney, really didn't like turning in two appraisal reports, just six months apart, and valuing the same asset at about half the value of the earlier appraisal. We told him that it was only an opinion, but he didn't want to hear that. He made me write a monograph on the changes in the intangible markets and their impact on real property assets before he would pay our fee.

The Scope of the Appraisal

Once an appraiser has told you what he is appraising and the effective date of the appraisal, he is obligated to tell you the scope of the assignment, which means:

- the research he must undertake to solve the appraisal problem,
- his experience (or lack thereof) in solving similar problems,
- the generally recognized valuation approaches and methods that apply to the solution,
- the names and competence of the staff working on the problem, including who did what,
- the names and jobs of the people with whom he spoke to understand the data.

The scope section of the appraisal report should constitute a couple of paragraphs that make sense. Appraisers don't expect the reader to be an appraiser or an appraisal reviewer who knows our body of knowledge. However, if the scope of the appraisal doesn't make any sense to you, why should you believe the conclusion?

Several years ago, I was asked by a bank to appraise a proposed quartzite mine. I had never heard of quartzite, which is a high silica rock that can be ground with precision into industrial quality sand, but I was a licensed appraiser and the law didn't permit the bank to directly depend upon folks who knew about quartzite but were not state-licensed appraisers to give their opinion about market value.

In the "scope" I described that I completed the on-line "Quarryology 101" school from Pit and Quarry Magazine. I explained that I retained a qualified geologist to estimate the proven reserves of the deposit and I described what else I would do to value the real estate as enhanced by the quartzite still in the ground.

The bank was satisfied with the appraisal, but the borrower became mad at me when he couldn't get the amount of the loan he wanted. The bank was willing to loan 70% of the value of the real estate, but only 50% of the value of the business, which meant that the borrower in effect had to build and operate the mine before he made any money from the mine.

The banker didn't inform his client of the bank's leverage requirements until after the appraisal, which was why I caught hell. The borrower had hoped to cash out on the loan just based on his good idea. This was in the unenlightened, bad old days before financial engineering, when banks actually had underwriting standards, appraisers were seen as independent, unbiased analysts, and relatively few banks failed.

Highest and Best Use

Appraisals should almost always be based on the highest and best use of whatever is to be appraised. One of my recent clients was told by the Georgia D.O.T. that they needed a corner of his land to connect the newly constructed 17th Street Bridge to the interstate. Although they only wanted about ½ of an acre out of the 2.5 acres that my client owned, the take included about a third of a two-story office building. It is hard to lop off a third of a building and still have anything useful left, so the D.O.T. condemned the entire building.

My client had paid about $2,500,000 for the 40,000-sf building on the 2.5-acre site in the mid 1990s, or $62.50/sf of building, which, at the time, was a fair price. He spent another $1,000,000 or so to rehabilitate the building and make it suitable for his business.

Once the 17th St. Bridge was constructed, land prices in this neighborhood went through the roof. Donald Trump bought a couple of acres almost across the street, and several other major developers made acquisitions of tracts of land big enough to support high rise, multiuse buildings. The market value of land had increased to $200/sf or about $8,700,000/acre. The D.O.T. paid about $4.3 million for the ½ acre they needed, but my client was annoyed because the D.O.T.

didn't pay anything for his building. D.O.T. had knocked the building down. Where was his just and adequate compensation for his building?

My client fired me when I didn't agree with him. The trouble between us was that his property had undergone a change in highest and best use. Land that for decades had been used to support two- and three-story, modest office buildings like the subject was now in demand for high rise buildings, just like the skyscrapers that now make up Atlantic Station on the western end of the 17th St. Bridge. Atlantic Station covers what had been the 138-acre Atlantic Steel Company brownfields site, another example of a change in highest and best use.

It is a little hard to feel sorry for my client. He was paid about $4,300,000 for what had cost him at most $3,500,000, and he still had a $17,000,000 property left after the new road construction was completed. On the other hand, he lost his building, he had to relocate his business, and he had to pay a capital gains tax on the condemnation award.

He wasn't in the real estate business, and he would have to sell the balance of the land to realize the benefit of the change in highest and best use. If he were to put up a "for sale" sign today he may have to wait a couple of years before he found a buyer, but the Fulton County Tax Commissioner now charges him $350,000/year in property taxes for what used to cost him $50,000/year. That annual property tax bill reflects a real cash flow obligation, whereas the $17,000,000 or so in real estate value for the remaining two acres is just potential wealth that is not generating any income. Like many before him my client became land rich, but cash poor.

Other Standards of Value

Market value is only one of the standards of value on which an appraiser may be asked to opine. Most of us who are homeowners are familiar with the idea of *insurance value*, which is likely to be limited to the part of the property that can be destroyed by fire or another insurable disaster. The land under the house often contributes about 20% of the total value of the real estate, so *insurance value* would exclude the contributory value of the lot.

I've been asked to help a client identify *investment value* when the client was considering bidding for an asset or in selling his business. I've even appraised the *sound value* of the possessory interest of a concessionaire in a National Park.

Sound Value is one of the strangest standards of value. *Sound Value* was defined by Congress as the lesser of *market value* (including the right to do business) or depreciated reproduction cost. Given the unusual circumstances of concessionaires at National Parks, *sound value* even makes some sort of common sense. After all, there is only one Yosemite National Park or only one Chattahoochee National Park and only one concessionaire for rafting through the park. The concessionaire's build-to-suit post and tenon buildings fit the ambiance of a rustic National Park. When the concessionaire's lease expires, he is entitled to be paid for his "possessory interest" in these specific buildings, not the value of a typical wood frame and drywall box that may have the same functional utility, but not comply with the standards imposed by the Parks Service.

None of an appraiser's usual tools apply very well to the appraisal of *sound value*. The rules for these appraisals require a detailed cost approach wherein the appraiser must consider the depreciated reproduction costs. The reproduction cost technique requires that the appraiser price out the cost to exactly reproduce the construction of the improvements, using the same or similar materials, as opposed to a replacement cost analysis that only requires that the appraiser estimate what it would cost to reproduce the functional utility of the improvements.

Think of the difference between the cost to construct a perfectly livable three-bedroom, two-bath brick, ranch-style house and a three-bedroom, two-bath castle complete with moat and turrets. They each may have 2,500 sf of living space, but the per-foot cost to construct for the brick ranch may be $85/sf and the cost to construct the castle may be $475/sf. Congress requires that the appraiser consider the reproduction costs of the concessionaire's buildings. In fact, the rules require that the appraiser hire a qualified cost estimator rather than making his own estimate using Marshall and Swift or RSMeans, both of which are costing manuals generally relied upon by appraisers.

National Parks and National Preserves are often in out of the way places. We were asked by the Parks Service to quote on an appraisal of the possessory interest for a concessionaire in the Smoky Mountains. These folks managed a remote, "rustic" lodge on the top of a mountain. Visitors hiked three hours up a mountain trail backpacking in all their baggage. Once a week a llama train packed in foodstuff and supplies. For us it was a ten-hour drive to get to the base of the mountain and then a three-hour climb up to inspect the property.

As unreasonable as it seems, my employees would not make the 20-hour round-trip drive and the six-hour climb up and back unless they were to be paid for their time. This additional overhead plus the cost for the third-party costing expert pushed our quote to the neighborhood of $25,000. One other knowledgeable appraiser quoted about the same, but someone who had never undertaken this type of assignment quoted about $10,000 and was hired.

In this case the concessionaire thought that the Parks Service appraiser did a lousy job, and, as was their right, hired their own appraiser – us. I am too old for three-hour hikes up a mountain, but one of our younger staff appreciated the assignment, and we all appreciated the fee.

Chapter 10: Appraising Interesting Holes in the Ground[5]

Caves

Lawyers often have the need for the solution of unusual appraisal problems. I got a call from an attorney who needed to know the value of a cave. Actually, he needed to know the value of a 100-acre tract of land on which was located a very successful, 30-year-old, family-oriented, recreational tourist business.

Caves are relatively unusual real property assets. An undiscovered cave doesn't add to the value of the land within which it is located, because no one knows that it is there. It is just like the tree that falls in the forest when there is no one around – vibrations in the air, but no sound!

On the other hand, people have been touring developed caves as far back as we have had people. We probably used to live in caves. Many caves are very beautifully decorated with stalagmites and stalactites, flowstone, soda straws, helictites and other fascinating formations. Even undecorated caves are interesting, like the Mark Twain Cave in Hannibal, Missouri, where Tom Sawyer and Becky hid out from Injun Joe.

Most of the time there is only a limited relationship between the real estate and the business that may be conducted within that real estate. Certainly, that was the case for the relationship between PBW, Inc., and our landlord. If we paid the rent on time and didn't frighten the horses, our landlord didn't care what we did in the Class B, plain vanilla office space we rented on Peachtree Street. On the other hand,

---

[5] *The Appraisal Institute published an article I wrote on this same subject in the Spring 2009 Issue of* The Appraisal Journal. *This is a much less technical exposition of the appraisal problem.* Although this story is based on a real-world case, a reader should be aware that we have a responsibility to our clients to protect the confidentiality of any of their proprietary information. These dollar figures illustrate the appraisal issues but should not be interpreted as actual information about the business or real estate we appraised.

we would have been equally satisfied with any of hundreds of other 2,500 sf, relatively inexpensive offices with a Peachtree Street address and adequate parking.

The tourist attraction cave, however, is inextricably integral to the operation of the tourist attraction business associated with touring a cavern. Without the cave there would be no attraction. The converse is also true. If it were not for the thousands of visitors, the cave would have only a marginal value. The visitors come and leave their money because of the hundreds of billboards, the thousands of dollars in advertising, the fact that their parents enjoyed a visit to the caves when they were in school, the capital improvements to make the cave accessible, the staff of guides, ticket takers, photographers, clerks and restaurant workers.

The market generally recognizes this inextricable or symbiotic relationship between real estate and business by applying a percentage rent rather than a fixed-dollars per square foot ($/sf) rent as it does with office or ordinary commercial space. Percentage rents are often applied in shopping centers and malls and for restaurants.

The cave in question had been drawing visitors for over 30 years. They could expect about 250,000 visitors per year, each of whom spent about $25 for admission, pictures, lunch, soft drinks, Dippin' Dots, and the right to sluice for gold and gemstones (each bag of mining soil guaranteed at least one gem or speck of gold). The business of operating the cave as a tourist attraction generated about $6,250,000 in gross revenues per year.[6]

The court case for which I was retained required both an appraisal of the real estate, including the contributory value of the developed cave, and a separate appraisal of the business operating the cave as a tourist attraction. The appraisals were required for a petition to partition the real estate and for an oppressed shareholder suit.

I was a newly minted Certified Business Appraiser (CBA), but I knew a very experienced business valuation testifying expert, Dr. Don

---

[6] Remember, these dollar values are made up for the purposes of illustration. They do not reflect the actual financials associated with this property.

Minyard, CBA, BVAL, CFE, CPA and ABV. I had met Don at the Institute of Business Appraisers' (IBA) weeklong seminar for testifying experts. This course was the best adult education I have ever experienced. The two instructors and course authors were Michele Miles, Esq., and Steve Schroeder, CBA. Michele had been a litigator for many years before becoming the IBA's Executive Director. Her father, Raymond Miles, had started the IBA in the 1970s.

Steve Schroeder graduated from law school but had the good sense to make his career as a business appraiser. Steve is one of the best respected appraisers in the country and is a Fellow of the IBA and on its Board of Directors. He has the added advantage of having read almost every bad appraisal report ever written.

The IBA requires that an applicant for the CBA designation submit two appraisal reports that demonstrate the applicant's mastery of the techniques and methods that a business appraiser employs to solve the business appraisal problem. Several of us CBAs had been commissioned as demonstration report reviewers. We were the first line of defense for the CBA designation. We could approve a report, but we couldn't turn one down without Steve's review. We would have to write a detailed critique, documenting each error with a citation to the relevant section of IBA's standards, and pointing out an appropriate solution using the body of knowledge literature. Steve would then read each rejected report and agree with or modify our decisions.

Over a 20-year history Steve read every error a business appraiser could make. He had no difficulty finding problems with the appraisal reports we had submitted in advance of our week together. Steve and Michele distributed our reports to others in the class whose job was to find any weakness that could be exploited to discredit the appraiser in court.

In class each of us had to undergo voir dire, prepare and present a demonstrative exhibit, do direct testimony, withstand cross-examination and finally sit at the table to advise the attorney during cross-examination. We would be critiqued after each session. Each of us thought highly of ourselves and of our work before we entered this class. Like most of my colleagues I had brought an appraisal with which I had won a court case. It didn't matter. Each of us wound up gutted, hanging in the meat locker. The whole experience was memorialized on videotape, so we could contemplate our sins at our leisure.

One of us had brought his prize-winning demonstration appraisal. He had been awarded $1,000 by the IBA for the best demonstration appraisal considered the year he had earned his CBA designation. He had really prepared a bulletproof appraisal report on a foundry business.

The primary method he used was called the public guideline method. This method is a part of the market approach and is based on a comparison of the subject business to publicly traded companies in the same or similar industry. If an appraiser can find three such publicly traded companies he can compare the publicly traded price-to-earnings ratio, sales-to-total invested capital, inventory turnover rates and other statistics from the public marketplace to his privately traded company and prepare an estimate of what the subject company would be worth if it were a publicly traded company. He then only has to account for the lack of marketability associated with a private company as compared to the open market for a publicly traded stock.

This method works well if the subject company is approximately the same size as the publicly traded company, usually within a factor of 10 times earnings or 10 times sales. It is surprising how many small companies are registered with the SEC and regularly file 10K and 10Q reports. Since all markets include some variance, the appraiser must have at least three publicly traded guideline companies to be certain that he is extracting a reasonable indication of the unit of comparison from the public marketplace.

Even though we know that we need three "comparables" to comply with the standard body of knowledge, in the real world when one finds two publicly traded guideline companies that are very close fits to the subject company, but only two, sometimes we go with what we have. My colleague went with two guideline companies, because that was all that there were.

In cross-examination Steve led the appraiser through the methodology he had used, which the appraiser explained with great authority. During the examination he acknowledged that he had relied on only two publicly traded companies for his data points, and he did a masterful job of explaining the closeness of fit and the research he had undertaken to compare the subject company to the two guideline companies and how he adjusted for differences.

In the process the appraiser admitted that the method would not have been applicable if he had found only one guideline company, but that with two that were so close to the subject and to each other, he had enough market support to rely on this method. It was the only method in his appraisal.

Don was called as a rebuttal witness. He explained that one of the guideline companies was in his hometown. In fact, Don had been called by the state's Attorney General to testify in the trial of the company's former chief financial officer, who was presently serving a sentence for fraud and embezzlement. It turns out that during the period for which the appraiser was relying on the 10K and 10Q reports for this company, the CFO was cooking the books and all the reports to the SEC were lies. At the time the appraiser prepared his report the story of the fraud was all over the news.

With that rebuttal testimony, the appraiser had to agree that his opinion was based on only one guideline company and was not reliable. He had to admit that he had not checked the news stories when he prepared his appraisal. Michele, who was in the role of the judge in this part of the class, ruled that the appraiser did not follow required due diligence procedures and instructed the jury to disregard all his testimony. She disqualified him as an expert (just as she found grounds to disqualify each of the rest of us during our turn).

To this day I don't know whether Don's rebuttal in that class was based on reality or was something he and Michele and Steve cooked up to show a weakness in the appraiser's methodology. When Don tells you something, he is believable. It is much more important to be believed than it is to be right when you are an expert witness.

Don is one of the most surprising people I have ever met. He has a very large, round head that sits almost directly on a somewhat round, short body. He has big round eyes with an open, trusting expression. He talks with a very broad Alabama drawl. Don's appearance does not strike fear in the heart of the opposing counsel or the opposing counsel's testifying expert, but it should. Were I to learn that I was up against Don on the other side of a case, my first piece of advice to the attorney who hired me would be to settle!

Don's Ph.D. degree is in Accounting, and he is a professor of accountancy. He is a Certified Fraud Examiner, as well as a CPA, CVA, CBA, BVAL. He put himself through graduate school by winning $65,000 on the TV game show "Scrabble," and in 2006 was a two-times champion on "Jeopardy." Don agreed to be responsible for the business valuation portion of our case about the cave, and I was to handle the real estate component.

The lawyer's problem was that the 100 acres including the cave had to be partitioned among the owners. The property was held as a tenancy-in-common or a "TIC." This is a form of ownership that creates an undivided interest (UDI) ownership among all the owners. The percentage of ownership may be specified; but, except for a distribution of any cash proceeds from the rental or sale of the property, even a 98% owner had no more rights than a 2% owner. It takes 100% of the ownership to sell or lease property owned as tenancy-in-common.

The family that owned the 100 acres as tenants in common found themselves in this position the way that most tenants in common become tenants in common. They inherited property. Tenancy in common is often called "heirs' property," and it occurs when a property owner dies without having made a will or when the decedent leaves the property "to my wife and my two children."

In this case, based on the laws of the state, the wife inherited a 50% UDI and each of the children inherited a 25% UDI. The land including the cave had been leased to the company operating the tourist business for 30 years, and the lease was coming up for renewal. It would take agreement of all three owners to renew the lease.

The life of these family members was further complicated by the fact that the daughter and her husband were not directly involved in the business of operating the cave tourist business. They owned a 25% interest in the business and they believed that they were not being treated fairly as minority stockholders.

Every state has made provision to rescue tenants-in-common through a process whereby a UDI owner can petition the court to partition the property. If, as is the case with the cave, the land cannot be partitioned into physically separate parts that represent the pro rata value equal to the pro rata ownerships, the property is sold, and the proceeds of the sale are divided according to the pro rata ownership.

The petition-to-partition process requires an independent appraisal of the real estate to be partitioned, which is why I was hired. The oppressed shareholder suit required a business appraisal, which is why Don was hired. Because the percentage rent to the real estate including the cave depended on the gross receipts to the tourist business, both appraisers had to agree on the total occupancy costs for the business, including the rent. Don and I combined our research and visited Moaning Caverns in California, Cave of the Winds in Colorado, Mark Twain Caverns, Meramec Caverns and Fantastic Caverns in Missouri, Diamond Caverns and Hidden River Cave in Kentucky, Ruby Falls in Tennessee, Luray Caverns in Virginia and Howe Caverns in New York as well as the seven show caves in Texas.

Among other things, we learned that percentage rent was a usual characteristic of properties when the owners of the real estate were not all the same parties that owned the cave tourist business. Sometimes percentage rent was based on gross receipts and sometimes it was based on turnstile revenues. For ease of calculation in the example below we based our estimate of market rent at 10% of total gross receipts.

To recap, assume that the cave company generated $6,250,000 in gross revenues and market rent for the real estate was 10% or $625,000. The income approach is based on the relationship between income (cash flow) and value, as we illustrated in the XYZ Grease and Tallow story. In the case of the cave, if we knew the capitalization rate (CAP) to apply to the $625,000 we could estimate the value of the real estate, including the contributory value of the cave. We solved the problem by partitioning the CAP into its component parts.

The return on real estate has consistently run between 8% and 10% over the last 50 years, even though rates have been a good deal lower since 2008. The land itself doesn't waste away. At the end of a lease the land is pretty much what it was at the beginning of the lease. Consequently, a 10% CAP rate on the land as if vacant may be reasonable, and it is easier to calculate 10% of something than to calculate 5.75% of something. The actual dollars in this book are for illustration purposes. It is the concepts that I find interesting.

Improvements, on the other hand, waste away. The bones of a building may last a long time, but the parts wear out. Roofs fail over about 20 years, the HVAC system lasts only about 15 years, a parking lot surface has about an eight-year life. Even the cave improvements wear out over time. The lighting system will fail. The water system will fail and must be replaced. If the CAP rate for the non-wasting vacant land is 10%, the CAP rate for the wasting improvements has to be enough more than 10% to return the capital represented by the wasting away of the improvements. This is what is meant by return of the capital.

Imagine a brand-new building with an expected useful life of 50 years. To recapture all the capital represented by that improvement one would need to recover $1/50^{th}$ of the value of the building each year, or 2%/year. Imagine a building that had a little age on it and a remaining useful life of 20 years. One would have to recover $1/20^{th}$ per year or 5% of the capital per year. The appropriate real estate CAP rate for a 20-year-old improvement would be 15% (10% return on capital plus 5% return of capital).

A CAP rate is the rate applied against value to estimate rent or applied against rent to estimate value. Depending on what you know or what you want to know, I=V*R (Income = Rate times Value) or V = I/R (Value equals Income divided by Rate) or R = I/V (Rate equals Income divided by Value). Once you know any two parts of the equation you can calculate the third.

To solve the real estate component of the cave problem we hired a competent local real estate appraiser who was very familiar with the market in the area of the cave. We asked him to estimate the value of the 100 acres and the surface improvements under the assumption that they had a useful economic purpose as a ranch plus a restaurant and a retail shop, but to ignore the contribution of the cave. The appraiser said that the real estate value (capital) was worth $1,750,000 without considering the contribution of the cave. He said that the 100 acres was worth about $10,000/acre as ranch land in that neighborhood, or $1,000,000 and that the improvements would contribute another $750,000 and had a remaining useful life of 20 years.

Assuming the ranch land would not change in value over time other than by inflation in the economy, we agreed that a 10% CAP rate for the land was reasonable, or $100,000/year rent ($1,000,000 * 10% = $100,000).

We thought that 10% was a reasonable return on the $750,000 represented by the capital contribution of the improvements, or $75,000/year rent, but we had to recover an additional 5%/year to represent the wasting of that asset over the 20-year remaining life, or an additional $37,500/year.

The total annual income from the land and improvements part of the real estate asset (after taxes and real estate related operating expenses) amounts to $212,500/year, excluding the contribution of the cave. The "landlord" was collecting $625,000/year income based on 10% of the gross receipts of the tourist business.

We could account for $212,500 of that income associated with the $1,750,000 worth of real estate other than the cave, which works out to a CAP rate of $212,500 / $1,750,000 or 12.14% for the traditional components of the real estate. The remaining $412,500/year real estate rental income must be associated with the contribution of the developed, tourist attraction cave.

Now that we knew the amount of annual income associated with the cave component of the real estate, all we had to do was estimate the appropriate CAP rate to apply to that stream of income to value the contribution of the improved cave as part of the real estate. Since the income to the real estate was very closely tied to the tourist attraction business, the risk associated with the $412,500 must also be closely associated with the risks of running that business.

Developing CAP rates for privately held businesses is an art and science of its own, but most of us are familiar with the idea that a business will typically sell at a multiple of its earnings. Small businesses, those under $10,000,000, usually sell between 3X and 5X earnings according to Tom West's *Business Broker's Resource Handbook*. A CAP rate is just the inverse of a multiple, so a 3X earnings is equal to a 33.3% CAP rate and a 5X earnings is equal to a 20% CAP rate.

Don worked out a reasonable business value CAP rate to apply to the intangible business earnings at about 30%. All we had to do was peg the CAP rate to the cave somewhere reasonably between the 12.14% real estate CAP rate (excluding the cave) and the business CAP rate of 30%.

Assuming that the appropriate CAP rate for the business of running the cave was 30%, a reasonable CAP rate for the $437,500 excess income associated with the caverns as real property might be about 25%, or slightly lower than for the intangible business asset, but a lot higher (more risky) than for the traditional parts of the real estate. At a 25% CAP rate, the $437,500 indicates a contributory value of the cave of $412,500 / 25% = $1,650,000.

The overall value of the real estate would be $1,750,000 for the land and surface improvements plus $1,650,000 for the improved cave, or $3,400,000. This was the "answer" being sought by the court.

One Good Cave Deserves Another Cave; Glenwood Caverns

Shortly after we had finished the work on the Texas cave, I got a call about a cave in Glenwood Springs, Colorado. A young couple had reopened a cave that had first been developed as a tourist attraction in 1895 by a local attorney, Charles W. Darrow, who was Clarence Darrow's father. The cave was one of the first to have electric lights, which were installed by 1897. The Darrow family operated "The Fairy Cave" until 1917. In 1999 the new owners discovered another 15,000 linear feet of active or "living" caverns and reopened the caves as the Glenwood Springs Caverns.

The basic problem faced by both the Darrows and, eighty years later by the new owners, had to do with getting the visitors to the cave during the seven months of the year that it is likely to snow in Colorado. The new owners' solution was to build an aerial tramway that would cross the river and bring tourists up to the top of Iron Mountain. They thought that the ride and the view of the canyon would bring enough customers to support a restaurant, even if they didn't want to tour the cave. They went to their bank with the idea and the bank called us, we now being world-renowned cave appraisers.

My associate, Kari Lazarova, ASA, CFA, and I visited the cave and reviewed the plans and specs for the proposed tramway and restaurant and reviewed three years of the operating history for the cave as a tourist attraction. We prepared an "as is" and "as if" appraisal for the cave business and real estate. The new owners built not only the tramway and restaurant, but also a toboggan run along the edge of the mountain and a swing that swung about 200' over the edge of the cliff. When they sold the operation a few years ago, they more than doubled the value of their investment.

Wells

Wells are another of the holes in the ground I've appraised over the years. Wells don't take up a lot of real estate, but they can produce a surprising amount of water and can be worth a surprising amount of money. In one case the appraisal came about because a publicly minded citizen in Franklin Springs, Georgia, wanted to donate a well on her property and the City of Franklin Springs very much wanted the water to service about 95 nearby families. Although Mrs. Johnson wanted to donate her interest in the well to the city, she wanted to be able to document the gift for her income tax return. Consequently, she needed an appraisal acceptable to the IRS.

In another case the City of Euharlee, Georgia, very much wanted the water from Mr. Clift's springs. Before Mr. Clift and the city could consummate the deal, the Georgia Power Company condemned Mr. Clift's pasture, including the springs. The well added substantially to the value of the pasture, and Mr. Clift wanted Georgia Power to pay fair market value for all the property taken in the condemnation, including the spring. Consequently, he needed an appraisal that included the contributory value of the spring and an appraiser willing to testify.

Neither the cost approach nor the sales-comparison approach to value is of much help in appraising a well. Municipal water authorities often buy and sell either treated or treatable potable water to each other, and in all the instances wherein I have appraised a well, I was able to find persuasive evidence about the wholesale market price for the water.

The usual unit of measurement for water is in thousands of gallons per day dependable supply. There may also be some estimate of the expected duration of the water flow. Engineers are the authoritative source for this estimate of "proven" capacity, which sets the upper limit on the earnings potential for the water supply.

The next most important variable that the appraiser must estimate is demand for the water. This usually depends on the number of households living near enough to the water source to make the costs of constructing the infrastructure to get the water to the users economically feasible. The entity that is the likely purchaser of the wholesale water is usually the best source for this type of information, but the appraiser also has an obligation to undertake enough research to satisfy him that the potential user's figures are reasonable.

Potential potable water sources don't require a lot of capital or operating expenses, but they require some. The appraiser must amortize the costs to drill the well and protect the wellhead or to capture the water from a spring, and there may be capital costs to pipe the water from the wholesaler to its buyer, but these are usually paid by the purchaser. There is likely to be a pumping station to be amortized and the wholesaler may have to pay the energy costs to operate the pumps, but these also may be paid for by the entity purchasing the water. The point is that the appraiser may have to deduct some operating expenses from the anticipated cash flow associated with the sale of the water.

The final variable the appraiser must determine is the appropriate capitalization rate and the appropriate capitalization model to apply to the expected net cash flow anticipated. I have always preferred a multiperiod capitalization model for a water source over a single period capitalization model. I talked about the simplest income approach valuation model in the chapter on the rendering factory and the cave. That is the "IRV" model (Income is equal to Rate times Value). In a multiperiod model the forecast net cash flow for each period (usually a period is a year) is discounted to a present value and the present values are summed over the expected forecast.

Present value theory is a standard part of everyday finance. If you and I agreed that I would loan you a dollar today and that you would pay me back a year from now at a 10% annual simple rate of interest prepaid, you would give me $0.10 (interest) today and owe me $1.00 (capital) in a year. I would in effect only be out $0.90 today. Consequently, the present value of $1.00 to be paid in one year is $0.90, assuming 10% simple interest. If we assume compound interest, the present value is actually $0.9091 given annual compounding. The present value factor formula for each year of the cash flow forecast is $1/(1+i)^n$ wherein $i =$ the annual rate of interest and $n =$ the number of the year. The further in the future the expected payment, the smaller is the present value of a dollar to be collected in that future year. Using the example above of a

10% interest rate, which appraisers call a discount rate, the present value of a dollar paid in the 10th year is $0.3855.

The present value of a future payment gets rather small as one goes out further and further in time. Using the example above the PV of $1.00 to be paid at the end of the 15th year is $0.2394. The PV of $1.00 paid at the end of the 20th year is $0.1485. At the end of the 25th year it is $0.0923 and at the end of the 30th year it is only $0.0573. The PV goes down dramatically as the discount rate increases. If the discount rate in the example above was 12%, the PV of $1.00 in 30 years it is $0.0334, which is almost a 42% reduction in PV for that year given a 20% increase in the estimate of the risks associated with the cash flow estimates.

The whole point of the paragraph above is that as the estimate of the time and risks increase, the consequence of an error in the forecast is reduced. The most valuable cash flows are the ones to be received sooner rather than later. In the multiperiod capitalization (or DCF for discounted cash flow) model the appraiser specifies the expected cash flows for each year of the analysis, accounting for expected changes in income and operating expenses and periodic capital expenses in the year that they are expected to occur.

Chimney Rock, NC

Sometimes the hole in the ground is a hole in the air. For over 100 years the same family owned Chimney Rock, which is the 535-million-year-old monolith on 1,000 acres adjacent to the Blue Ridge Parkway. In 1946, plans were drawn for an elevator to transport people to the top. A 198-foot tunnel was blasted into the mountain, as was a 258-foot elevator shaft. The family developed a hotel, a restaurant and other tourist-oriented amenities. Tourists by the thousands came to ride to the top of the monolith and enjoy the 75-mile view of the Blue Ridge Parkway.

In 2007 the Family agreed to sell Chimney Rock to the State of North Carolina. Three competent real estate appraisers valued the 1,000 acres containing the tower. These three valued the land using sales of large acreage mountain tracts. They added the value of the hotel and other buildings based on the income, sales comparables and cost approaches to value. All three acted independently. Each came to a number reasonably close to the number estimated by the other two. None of the numbers reflected the value that the family believed was a reasonable value for their asset. The state was willing to pay whatever value could be supported, but they could not pay more than *market value* for Chimney Rock.

There is only one Chimney Rock. There was only one possible willing seller. The support for *market value* was going to come down to the opinion of appraisers. The family hired me to review the real estate appraisals and help them understand why the value judgments were coming up with a number that was so much lower than what they thought their property was worth.

I thought that the real estate appraisers had each done a credible job and had come to a reasonable conclusion about the value of the real estate. What they had not appraised, and what they were neither trained nor experienced in appraising, was the contributory value of the Chimney Rock tourist business as a going concern. The real estate was an essential component of the enterprise, but it was not the whole story. The real estate appraisals did not capture the contributory value of the years of advertising that had made Chimney Rock successful as a tourist designation. It didn't include the value of the skilled workforce. These were the intangible assets of the business that were not reflected by the real estate appraisals.

Most of the value in the real estate was the 1,000 acres of land in the park. Not all these acres were required to support the tourist business, and there was a contributory value of the excess land. The cash flow from the tourist business was not large enough to support the total value of the 1,000 acres, but it was more than enough to support the acres required for the tourist attraction.

Suppose, for example, the contributory value of the land was $10,000/acre and the tourist attraction required 50 acres or $500,000 worth of land. Also, assume that the reasonable return on the value of land was 10%, which means that $50,000 of annual cash flow from the operation of the tourist attraction had to be allocated as "rent" for the 50 acres of land. However, there was a lot of cash flow left over after allocating $50,000 for the land, paying all the staff, the utilities, the taxes and the other operating expenses. Consequently, there was every reason to believe that the enterprise had both tangible and intangible value. The enterprise included the hotel and the other buildings that were a part of the tourist attraction.

Once one reasonably partitioned the entire property into the part that was best valued as undeveloped land and the part that was best valued as a going concern, both the state and the family were able to agree to a transaction price. According to the Chimney Park website, chimneyrockpark.com/about-us/history/, the state purchased the park in 2007 for $24,000,000.

Mines

Mines are just another type of hole in the ground. There is a business element to a mine as well as a real estate element. The real estate can be considered as the surface rights for the portions of the land undisturbed by the mining process plus the real estate after reclamation, the value of the minerals in situ (still in the ground), and the value of the mineral lease, which is usually reflected as the present value of the royalty payment for the minerals once extracted.

The business component includes the right to mine the minerals, the machinery, equipment and working capital required to extract and process the minerals, the skilled workforce and the marketing required to turn the minerals into money.

Several different skills and professionals are usually required to value a mine. The real estate appraiser has a part to play, but so do the geologist, the machinery and equipment (M&E) personal property appraiser and the business appraiser. If the mine also includes a substantial store of materials inventory on site, the assignment may also require a materials appraiser as a part of the team.

It is reasonable to ask why anyone would want to appraise a mine?

I've been hired for assignments associated with a sale, an estate, eminent domain takings and for acquisition and development (A&D) loans.

Mineral Rights, Even When There Are No Minerals

In theory the rights of real estate ownership extend from the center of the earth to the top of the sky. According to Wikipedia, the tallest building in the world (so far) is the 2717 ft. tall Burj Khalifa in Dubai, United Arab Emirates. The Tau Tona Mine in the goldfields of Johannesburg reached some 2.4 miles underground, making it the deepest mine in the world. These presently constitute the physical constraints on the theoretical real estate rights.

The physical components of real estate can be subdivided into land and buildings, air rights, surface rights, and subsurface rights. One of the most usual subdivisions is to separate the mineral rights from the surface rights.

Often mining companies or speculators acquire the mineral rights on large acreage tracts. Sometimes merchantable (marketable) minerals were discovered, and sometimes they were not. However, once the mineral rights were severed from the balance of the fee (the whole bundle of rights), the real estate is generally considered inferior to a similar parcel that still has the whole bundle of rights.

Even if there are no minerals the severed mineral rights often have a value to the party who owns the balance of the rights on a particular tract of land. How concerned might you be if you knew that someone else had the right to dig up your front yard? What would you do if you learned that the bank would not make you a loan because you did not own the fee simple title to your property? All these scenarios have led to transactional evidence of the fact that the mineral rights have some value even if all the parties agree that there are no merchantable minerals to be mined.

The sales comparison approach is based on the economic principle of substitution, which is to say that a rational, economically motivated person will not pay more for the subject than he would for an alternative of equal utility. Generally, the appraiser selects reasonably comparable real properties that sold in a fair and open market and adjusts those sales to be more similar to the subject of his appraisal. The adjusted price of the comparables, using some standard unit of comparison such as price per acre, is employed to indicate the market value of the subject.

I believe that a sale of mineral rights wherein the value of the minerals-in-situ was not a factor is a good comparable sale for the type of severance that I have described above. That is, mineral rights were sold even if there were no proven reserves of marketable minerals. The motivation of the buyer was to perfect the title to the "surface" land, which really means to reassemble the entire bundle of rights. From the point of view of the seller, the asset being sold was the intangible asset of severed mineral rights. Even if there was a potential that the mineral rights sold contained merchantable minerals, they were no longer of economic value to the selling party.

In the market I was studying, I found 15 sales of mineral rights that appeared to me to be reasonable comparables for the severed mineral rights on the property I was appraising. The transaction prices ranged from a low of about $30/acre to a high of about $300/acre. What was most surprising was that there appeared to be two modal points, one about $50/acre and another at about $200/acre, rather than an array of sales evenly distributed throughout the range. Most of the buyers who paid the highest prices had an immediate need to reassemble the mineral rights with the balance of the property rights.

An Option Pricing Model

Often an appraiser cannot find enough sales that are reasonable comparables to the subject of the appraisal, and he or she must find another analogue from the marketplace. Another way to value mineral rights is an option-pricing model. An American option consists of the right (but not the obligation) to purchase an asset as of a certain date in the future for an established price. The party that holds the option pays a small price today, say $1.00, for the right to purchase the asset for a specific price, say $100, at some date in the future. If a year from now that asset is trading at $90, the option holder does not execute the option. He is out only the $1 he paid for the right to buy the asset for $100. On the other hand, if the asset is trading for $110 as of the option date, the owner of the option buys the asset for $100 "strike price" and makes $9 ($10 less the $1 he paid for the option).

If the costs to extract a ton of the mineral in question exceed the sales price of that mineral once extracted, the miner leaves the mineral in the ground until market price exceeds costs. This is the reason that many gold mines that were mothballed when gold was at $400/oz have been reopened once gold reached $1,500/oz or that oil wells that were considered productive when oil sold for $100/barrel are closed now that oil is at about $50/barrel.

An appraiser is always trying to use information that he does know to solve a problem when the information he wishes he knew is just not available. It is very hard to know what the market will pay for mineral rights when no one knows if there are any saleable minerals in that patch of ground. However, one can know the sales price of a mineral of a known quality and quantity once it is extracted and one can know the costs per cubic yard or ton required to extract that mineral.

Risk Analysis; Discount Rates

In theory the value of any asset depends on the present value of future benefits that will accrue from the ownership of that asset. Present value is a function of the expected holding period and the opportunity cost or discount rate. In determining the appropriate discount rate, the appraiser considers such factors as the level of interest rates offered by lenders, rates of return expected by investors on relevant investments, and the risk characteristics of the anticipated benefits.

The Build-up Method

Every equity discount rate includes the following elements: 1) a risk-free rate of return, 2) a general (equity) risk premium, and 3) an asset specific risk adjustment. In the build-up method the equity risk premium is typically obtained from the Ibbotson[7] data and needs to be consistent with the selection of the risk-free proxy. A discount rate that incorporates Ibbotson data is applied to after corporate tax equity net cash flow. Table 3 below presents the development of the equity discount rate for a theoretical asset as of the end of 2002 using the build-up method.

The most often-used analogue for the risk-free rate is the 20-year US Treasury security yield to maturity published by the Federal Reserve Board nearest the effective date of the appraisal used in this example.

The yield to maturity on the 20-year US Treasury bond as of December 30, 2002, was 4.83%. The general market equity premium of 7.4% was obtained from Ibbotson Associates *Stocks, Bonds, Bills, and Inflation Yearbook 2002 (SBBI 2002)*. The industry average premium for mining and quarrying nonmetallic minerals was a negative 3.43%, showing that mining companies were less risky than the market as a whole. On average, small companies have higher rates of return than larger companies. The size premium study, conducted by Ibbotson Associates, estimated an additional premium of 5.33% for the 10th decile of companies listed on NYSE. Thus, the estimated base equity premium before considering any subject's specific risk is 14%, rounded.

The unsystematic risk, also referred to as investor-specific risk, is a function of characteristics of the industry and the specific company. After considering the impact of the possible decrease in market demand, the financial performance of the subject, the level of competition in the industry, and the management of the business, we estimated the business-specific risk to be in the range of 3.5%-5.5%. The equity discount rate for the subject in this example, developed under the build-up method, is within the range of 18%-20%. We used the upper-end of the range (20%) in our analysis.

---

[7] *Stocks, Bonds, Bills and Inflation: 2001 Yearbook, Valuation Edition*, Ibbotson Associates, Chicago.

Table 3: Build-up of the Equity Discount Rate Using for the Subject Business

Components of the Required Holding Period Return	Lower	Higher	Source/Brief Rationale
Long-Term Government Bond Yield-to-Maturity	4.83%	4.83%	Yield as of December 30, 2002. The Fed H. 15 report as of December 30, 2002. See http://www.bog.frb.fed.us/releases/H15
+ Ibbotson Common Stock Premium	7.40%		See Ibbotson Associates SBBI Yearbook 2002 for annual premium returns.
+ Industry Premia, Mining & Quarrying of Non-metallic Minerals	-3.43%		See Ibbotson Associates SBBI Yearbook 2002 for annual premium returns, Table 3-5, p. 43.
+ Small Cap Stock Premium – 10-th Decile	5.33%		See Ibbotson Associates SBBI Yearbook 2002 for annual premium returns. Table 7-5, p. 125.
= Total Equity Premium	9.30%		
Base Holding Period Required Return	14.13%	14.13%	<> Base equity discount rate
Investor Specific Risk Premium(s) for This Entity:			
+ Market Demand	1.00%	1.50%	
+ Competition	1.00%	1.50%	
+ Subject's financial performance vs. the industry	1.00%	1.50%	
+ Management	0.50%	1.00%	
Total Investor Specific Risk Premium for This Entity	3.50%	5.50%	
Estimated Range of Required Holding Period Returns	17.63%	19.63%	
Estimated Range of Required Holding Period Returns	18%	20%	*Rounded*

The Capital Asset Pricing Model (CAPM)[8]

When representative comparative company data exists, the discount rate typically is determined from that comparative data using the CAPM model. The concept of the CAPM is that the cost of equity is equal to a risk-free rate plus beta times the general equity risk premium.

The basic CAPM formula is:

$$E(R_i) = R_f + \beta * (RP_m)$$
where:

$E(R_i)$ = expected return (cost of capital) for an individual security,

R_f = rate of return available on a risk-free security,

β = beta for the subject business,

RP_m = equity risk premium for the market as a whole.

Beta is a measure of the relative total return volatility of the publicly traded companies that are most similar to the subject as compared to the volatility of all common stocks of public companies. Total return includes dividends paid plus appreciation or depreciation in the price of the stock over a given time period. It is measured by comparing the return on an individual security with the return on the market as a whole as measured by a market index such as the S&P 500.

As it is applied, the benchmark portfolio having a beta of 1.0 is defined to be a diversified portfolio of common stocks such as the S&P 500. Stocks with beta greater than 1.0 have greater than average risk and stocks with beta less than 1.0 have less risk than the market. When beta is equal to zero, one assumes that the risk is zero, and the return that a zero-beta security is expected to earn is defined to be the risk-free rate.

---

[8] Much of the actual analysis for the CAPM is based on work by my former Associate, Kari Lazarova, ASA, CFA.

Treasury bonds and bills are used as proxies for the risk-free rate.[9]

The reason that the CAPM includes only systematic risk as a factor in determining the required rate of return is that, theoretically, holding a fully diversified portfolio of securities can eliminate unsystematic risk. The issue of beta is quite important for the subject, because – as a whole – our research shows that mining companies experience much less risk than the stock market.

As it is reasonable to believe that the industry average debt/equity ratio and the average beta derived from the selected guideline public companies would provide a reasonable estimate of the subject's cost of equity, we analyzed the performance of several of the largest publicly traded industrial mining companies.

Betas, published by the various financial reporting services, reflect the leverage of the respective publicly traded companies. The estimated effect of different levels of debt can be removed by unlevering the betas. The unlevered beta is relevered to reflect the target degree of leverage, which is typically the industry average debt/equity ratio.

The formula for unlevering beta is:

$$\beta_a{}^u = \frac{\beta_e{}^l}{}, \text{ where: equation (2)}$$

β_e = beta of the equity of the levered firm.

$\beta_a{}^u = 1 + (1- Tc) * D/E$, where:

$\beta_a{}^u$ = beta of the assets of the firm. This is also the beta of the equity of the firm unlevered.

T_c = corporate tax rate

D/E = debt-to-equity ratio of the levered firm

[9] Source: Fishman, Jay; Pratt, Shannon; Griffin, J.; Wilson, D., and Meltzer, Stanton. *Guide to Business Valuation*. Practitioners Publishing Company, 1999.

The following is a group of seven publicly traded companies that we used as proxies for risk for the mining and quarrying industry:

Table 4: Guideline Public Companies

Company Name	Ticker	b_e^l	Total Debt in $M	Market Cap. in $M	Total Debt/Equity	b_a^u
Vulcan Materials Company	VMC	0.60	936	3,846	0.24	0.51
Martin Marietta Materials, Inc.	MLM	0.70	909	1,583	0.57	0.51
Lafarge North America, Inc.	LAF	0.90	1,197	2,114	0.57	0.66
Florida Rock Industries, Inc.	FRK	0.50	114	1,105	0.10	0.47
Texas Industries, Inc.	TXI	0.70	444	519	0.85	0.45
Centex Construction Products, Inc.	CXP	0.30	100	652	0.15	0.27
CRH Plc (ADR)	CRHCY	1.10	4,484	6,301	0.71	0.72
					0.50	
					average b_a^u	0.51
					Target D/E	0.50
					Subject b_e^l	0.69

Source: Hoover's and SEC filings as of December 31, 2002.

The average beta unlevered for the guideline companies is 0.51. We applied the industry target leverage ratio of 33% debt and 67% equity to the subject business.[10] We estimated that the beta for the subject is 0.69. We used this beta in equation (1) to arrive at the equity discount rate for the subject business. Details of the equity discount rate calculation are presented in Table 5:

Table 5: CAPM Cost of Equity

Risk-free rate (Rf)	4.83%
+ Market Premium (Rm)	7.40%
x Subject $b_e{}^l$	0.69
= r_k (%) industry	9.94%
+ small cap stock premium	5.33%
+ company specific risk	4.50%
= equity discount rate	19.77%
= r_k (%) rounded	20.0%

You can see that in the examples above, both the build-up rate method and the capital asset pricing model (CAPM) indicate that the equity discount rate for the subject is 20%.

Weighted Average Cost of Capital

If the job of the appraiser is to appraise the total company (both debt and equity), the risk rate for an asset must reflect its total capital structure (both debt and equity). The Weighted Average Cost of Capital (WACC) is a blended discount rate that reflects the costs of capital.

---

[10] The respective market values of debt and equity are used. The outstanding book value of debt is assumed to be equal to market value of debt.

Each component of the capital structure is weighted to arrive at the *subject's* weighted average cost of capital. Table 6 shows calculations of the weighted average cost of capital (WACC) for a specific company at 14.5%:

Table 6: WACC Calculation

Cost of Capital	Weight	Rate	WACC
Cost of Equity -target industry ratio	0.67	20.0%	13.40%
Pre-tax Cost of Debt - target industry ratio	0.33	5.35%	
Tax rate		40.0%	
After-tax Cost of Debt		3.21%	1.06%
WACC			14.46%
WACC Rounded			14.5%

Bolt Holes

Enough about appraising holes in the ground and the stuff that may or may not be in them. You have probably read more than you ever wanted to know about the way that an appraiser may form an opinion about the value of these unusual assets. Well, almost enough. I want to tell one more story about a very unusual set of holes in the ground and, I think, an unusual solution to the value of these holes. This was before my time, but the appraiser hired to undertake the assignment was my mentor, Jim Pritchett.

Atlanta has the beginnings of a subway system called The Metropolitan Atlanta Rapid Transit Authority (MARTA). Much of the downtown portion of this line is a tunnel bored through the granite ridge on which downtown Atlanta sits. The Peachtree Center Station is 120 feet below the surface. Because the station itself was built within the Peachtree Street right-of-way, MARTA didn't have to acquire any subsurface rights from any of the private property owners who had built Atlanta's downtown skyscrapers that line Peachtree Street.

Once the tunnel for the station had been drilled, the engineers determined that they needed to protect the surface of the granite from spalling and falling off into the tunnel. The architects wanted to preserve the natural granite as the interior finish for the station. The solution was to drill bolt holes into the sides of the tunnel and installing bolts and large surface washers to keep the surface of the rock intact.

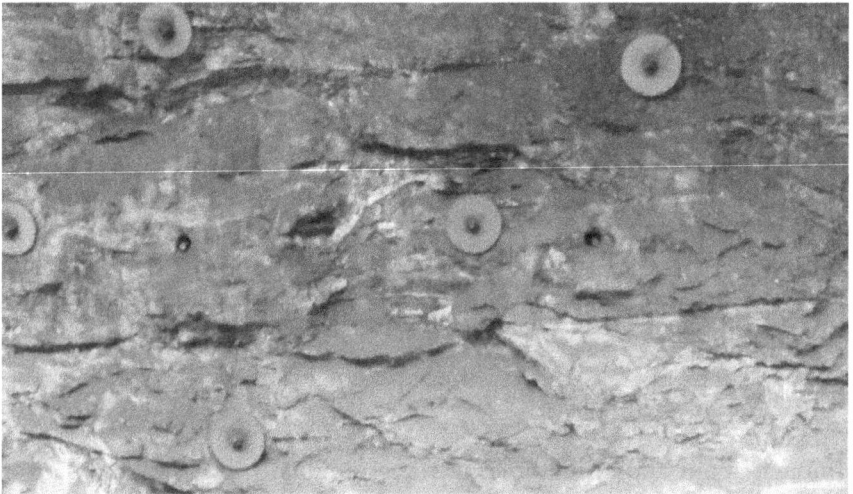

The trouble was that the city had already used all the right of way that it owned for the tunnel, and the bolt holes would have to extend into the property of the skyscrapers. MARTA had the authority to condemn the bolt holes using eminent domain. The problem was to determine the just and adequate compensation to be paid to the private property owners.

The buildings along Peachtree Street all had basements and subbasements, and all were anchored in the same granite bedrock through which the tunnel had been drilled. Probably the deepest subbasement was about 50 feet below the surface, or about 70 feet above the roof of the tunnel.

The usual method an appraiser uses to partition the fee simple rights to land is to consider the theoretical functional limits to the utility of the land. If one is not considering the mineral rights, the subsurface rights are the right to build a basement or foundation sufficient to support a building that would develop the site to its highest and best use.

That generally means up to 60' of subsurface, the development potential of the surface, and the air rights that would represent the tallest building that the market would support. Atlanta's tallest building is the 1,023' high 55-story Bank of America Tower between Peachtree Street and West Peachtree Street at North Avenue and was the 9th-tallest building in the U.S. at the time I wrote this section.

Clearly the rock through which the bolt holes would be drilled was outside the column of rights that was otherwise useful to the land owners. Just and adequate compensation is based on the value to the owner, not the value to the entity that is acquiring the property. It is reasonable to say that the market would pay $200/sf for the land that the property owner owns. It is not reasonable to say that "but for" the 400 cubic feet of rock that MARTA needs for a bolt hole, the $45-million station could not be used, so the value of the bolt holes must be some fraction of $45 million.

Jim's solution to the appraisal problem was to estimate the costs in time and money that a property owner would have to pay to sue MARTA for not having paid just and adequate compensation for a bolt hole, and he based his opinion of value on the expected cost of a suit as the best analogue for the real estate value of the bolt holes. He turned in his appraisal, and no one sued.

Chapter 11: Getting from Here to There – Corridor Appraisals

One Foot on a Power Pole

Sometimes the real value of real property is that it provides a corridor that can get you from here to there. Such was the case for the Southern Company, which is the holding company for Georgia Power, Alabama Power, Gulf Power and other power companies in the southeastern United States.

Prior to 1996 power companies generally permitted cable television companies to attach their cables to a power pole. The parties negotiated a modest attachment charge. At that time the cable television (CATV) companies were "Mom and Pop" operations and the power companies were massive utilities. The 1996 Telecommunications Act mandated that cable television companies had the right to attach their cables to existing power poles.

About two-thirds of what we call telephone poles are really owned by the power companies, and most of the rest are owned by telephone companies. Both these utilities have had sharing agreements for years permitting the power companies to attach to telephone poles and telephone companies to attach to power poles. The rents for any imbalance in the use of the other party's poles are negotiated periodically between the power company and the phone company.

Of course, no one cared for the right to attach a cable to one power pole. What mattered was the right to attach to the whole corridor of poles that lead from the CATV station to the customers' houses. CATV is not unique in its interest in a corridor.

Rail Lines

Rail lines are among our oldest corridors. More modern corridors include the underground pipelines and fiber optics.

Just this last year I was asked by an appraiser friend to help value 60 miles of a privately held, short-line railroad. A fellow in South Georgia had bought a little-used railroad and was using it to store rolling stock. With the economic downturn the major railroads had many more boxcars and engines than they needed, and they had to put the unused stock someplace. This fellow was renting parking space for a few dollars per day per boxcar and was making so much money that he was building spur lines wherever he had the space.

A local bank had loaned the fellow much of the cost of the acquisition. In support of the loan the fellow produced an appraisal of the tangible assets prepared by a local real estate appraiser and a nationally recognized railroad machinery and equipment personal property appraiser. The local real estate appraiser had done a reasonable job of valuing the mostly rural land through which the railroad corridor ran but had not appraised any of the in-town lands or any of the buildings owned by the railroad. The M&E appraiser had prepared a typical, three-page report that just listed the tangible assets (numbers of rails, tons of ballast, number of cross ties, rolling stock owned by the railroad, etc.) and included prices for each class of asset. The bank's regulators stated that neither the land appraisal nor the personal property appraisal met USPAP requirements. If the bank didn't want to write off this loan, the appraisals would have to be written to comply with USPAP.

Lots of loans in the rural areas of Georgia are made between good old boys, often with only a wink or a nod in the direction of some banking regulation imposed from afar. In this case all the parties involved knew each other and all were perfectly happy with the loan. The only fly in the ointment was that the bank regulator was coming, which meant that the appraisal had to comply with USPAP.

USPAP (and the Appraisal Institute) make it possible for a real estate appraiser to accept professionally prepared reports by other experts so long as the real estate appraiser understands the report and is willing to accept full responsibility for the other expert's report. We are often obligated to accept reports prepared by environmental engineers or land use planners and architects as we make decisions about the property's highest and best use. In the case of the personal property appraisal of the railroad we believed that we needed to see the backup materials that were the foundation for the M&E appraiser's opinion.

This is where things began to get a little sticky. It seems that the borrower had neglected to pay the balance of the railroad appraiser's fee. After all, he got his loan and it was less expensive to be sued by some guy from Idaho than it was to pay the fee. My pal Joe ought to have learned something from this, but he didn't get a retainer and "too soon old and too late smart." The banker persuaded the borrower to pay the balance of the M&E appraiser's fee, who then sent us about 150 pages of backup data. M&E appraisers really do a lot of work even if their reports don't necessarily reflect the magnitude of their research. Once we were persuaded that the M&E appraiser knew what he was talking about, we could accept his report and incorporate his values as a part of our report.

The remainder of the assignment was straightforward enough, so long as one is willing to accept the concept of an "across the fence" appraisal. An "across the fence" appraisal works well for corridors like railroad rights of way and underground pipeline rights of way. For these appraisals the appraiser ignores the fact that the subject is 100' wide and 300 miles long and pretends that it is an undifferentiated component of the surrounding land. If the subject is a 100'-wide rail corridor through a 500-acre pasture, one appraises the value of the pasture land per square foot or per acre and assigns that as the value of that portion of the rail corridor. In an eminent domain assignment, the appraiser may have to also determine whether the rail corridor "damages" the remainder of the land through which it passes, but more on what happens when the government wants your land in a later section of this book.

An "across the fence" appraisal wouldn't solve the valuation problem for the power pole attachment case. The power poles were themselves "attachments" to the ground and the power company owned an easement (usually obtained from the local government or the highway department) to install the power poles in the first place. Once the pole was erected it became real property owned by the power company.

The Fifth Amendment to the U.S. Constitution reads in part: *nor shall private property be taken for public use, without just compensation.* The 11th U.S. Circuit Court ruled that the mandated right to attach, established by the Telecommunications Act of 1996, constituted a "taking" under the meaning of the Fifth Amendment (eminent domain) clause of the Constitution. The question then became "what is fair market rent for the right to attach a cable to a power pole?" The attorneys for the Southern Company hired us to develop evidence of the appropriate charge.

There actually is market-based evidence for the rental of a corridor. Not much evidence, I admit, but some. I suppose I should not be too surprised, in spite of the fact that the rental of one foot of a power pole sounds like an unusual real estate rental. If something in fact has value, the market will find a way to price it, no matter how unusual that asset may be.

I found that the Massachusetts Transit Authority (MTA) leases access to the subway walls to fiber optic companies and MARTA leases attachment to the side of the MARTA rails to fiber optic companies at dollars per foot. The Florida Turnpike Authority leases access to the interstate median for cell tower companies. Interstate pipeline companies have leased unused pipelines for similar fiber optic transmissions. I even found a few situations wherein power companies or telephone companies leased access to poles to security firms for hard-wired alarm systems.

All the market examples for corridor rentals came from the unregulated private enterprise marketplace. Unfortunately for the

Southern Company, power poles and CATVs are regulated by the Federal Government. The Federal Communications Commission (FCC) says grace over the CATV industry, and the Federal Energy Regulatory Commission (FERC) regulates the electric power industry. The FCC claimed jurisdiction, which meant that the power companies were in for a rough ride. I think that if the case had been heard by the FERC, the CATV industries would have fallen into the power company's cook pot.

The standard utility pole is 40' in length and is usually buried 6' in the ground. The top section of the pole is called "the supply space" and is used for the power transmission lines and transformers and other electricity stuff. This can occupy 6' to 8' of the pole. The next space is called "the safety zone" and is about 6' of space below the transmission lines to provide an area wherein workers can safely work on all of the lines on a pole. Below that are a couple of feet wherein the telephone company attaches its lines and the CATV company gets one foot. Remember, 8' of the pole is in the ground and the lowest line must be about 20' above the ground. Consequently, it is easy to run out of pole.

Because the power companies' rates are regulated by each state and because the rates are closely associated with proven operating and capital costs, power companies maintain very accurate and detailed records about the cost to acquire, install and maintain the power poles. In this case I thought it would be reasonable to use a cost approach to the valuation problem.

We knew the costs to acquire and install the poles. We knew the average life of a pole in each area. We knew the annual maintenance costs and we knew the share of the useful space required by each attacher. I postulated that all attachers had an equal stake in the 26' of the pole required to support the pole in the ground and raise the height of the lowest line to the appropriate distance above the ground. I assigned the costs of the "useful" space wherein all attachers could attach to the pole on a pro rata basis. I came up with an average annual total "rent-use" for a utility pole of about $125/year, if memory serves, and determined that the CATV company's fair share was about $38/pole.

The CATV companies objected to the proposed approximately 500% rate increase from the approximately $7/pole that the FCC had approved with no appraisal evidence prior to the 1996 Telecommunications Act. The FCC approved rate had been set in the 1960s when CATV companies were a nascent industry. The $7/pole rate didn't pay any attention to either replacement costs, maintenance costs or the unusable space on a pole. The FCC turned down the increase and the case went back to the 11th Circuit Court of Appeals, which had originally ruled that the 1996 Act constituted a "taking."

Courts change and change opinions over time. By November 2002 the 11th Circuit ruled:

> *It is well settled that if the government commits a taking, it is under an obligation to put the aggrieved party in the position it was in before the taking occurred (and no better). In unique cases such as this one, marginal cost meets this test-unless, of course, the aggrieved party proves lost opportunity by showing (1) full capacity and (2) a higher valued use. APCo never alleged these facts. Therefore, its challenges based on the Fifth Amendment and the Administrative Procedure Act must fail, and its petition for review is denied.* (C.A.11,2002. Alabama Power Co. v. F.C.C. 311 F.3d 1357, Util. L. Rep. P 14,438, 16 Fla. L. Weekly Fed. C 63.

The court ruled that the one foot of space that the CATV required on the pole was "nonrivalrous" property. In other words, they believed that even if the power company owned the pole and even if the 1996 Act resulted in a taking of the power company's property, the power company didn't need the property so – no harm, no foul.

In a related case brought by Gulf Power, another subsidiary of the

Southern Company, *National Cable & Telecommunications Assoc. v. Gulf Power Co.*, the issue had changed slightly because the CATV company was now providing internet services. The 1996 Act said nothing about the internet, and the power company believed that this gave them a superior argument to limit CATV companies just to television. If they wanted to attach wireless antennas and internet they would have to negotiate new and possibly unregulated attachment agreements with the power companies. The 11th Circuit ruled in Gulf Power's favor in 2000, but the U.S. Supreme Court reversed that decision in 2002 and left the FCC in charge. I was pleased to be cited in a U.S. Supreme Court decision, even if they rejected me lock, stock and barrel.

I don't know whether there is any other end to this story. At this time Linda became ill and I had to drop out of the case. The lawyer with whom I worked no longer works on this issue and didn't know the present status of the dispute. Not knowing the outcome of a dispute in which I have provided testimony is the rule for me, not the exception. My job is to tell the truth as I see it and leave before closing arguments. I did stay for closing arguments once, and once was enough. That lawyer on the other side said things about me I would not want my momma to hear.

Chapter 12: They Can't Do That to Me. Can They?

Eminent Domain

What's mine is mine unless the government wants it. Most of the time, so long as we pay our taxes, most of us in the U.S. live out our allotted time with relatively little interference from the intrusions of government. We are so little concerned that most of the time most of us don't even vote. However, every so often some of us find ourselves in front of a bulldozer. Our property could be in the way of a road widening, a reservoir, an airport runway expansion, a school or the myriad other "public purposes" that dot our landscapes.

The Kelo case in Connecticut (Kelo vs. City of New London, 545 U.S. 469 (2005)) was the first time in my career as an appraiser that eminent domain became a viable public issue. The 5th Amendment to the U.S. Constitution concludes with the clause *"nor shall private property be taken for public use, without just compensation."*

In many states and local communities, the interpretation of "public use" had grown to include the taking of private property by public entities for use by other private parties under the interpretation that economic development constitutes a public use. I remember a situation in Henry County, Georgia, where a local pharmacy on a corner location was condemned so Walgreens pharmacy chain could construct a superstore. The reason that the Development Authority gave for their condemnation of private property for another private purpose was that the bigger store would pay more property tax and would hire more employees than the Mom and Pop store.

In 2005 the U. S. Supreme Court approved New London's taking of Mrs. Kelo's house on a bluff overlooking the harbor. She had refused to sell to a developer who proposed a major, new project. The developer had convinced the city that the project would bring in over $1.2 million in taxes and hire over 3,000 people. As it turned out after the house was moved and dozens of other houses were demolished, the developer's business failed and the site was eventually used as a city dump.

Once the Kelo case made the national news, many people, including state legislators, began to reconsider the fairness of their earlier interpretation of *public use*. We the people thought that private property was supposed to belong to the people who owned it until they wished to sell.

Although it might be acceptable to condemn property for a new road or a new school, just because someone wanted my property to build a skyscraper or new shopping center wasn't sufficient reason to take my property unless I was willing to sell, and the potential buyer agreed to my price.

There are many examples of a hold-out property owner being paid many times the typical seller's price because a developer needed that last parcel to complete his project. Most of us thought that the windfall was the holdout's good fortune, and that it was unfair for the government to step in and force the holdout to sell or take his property and just pay *market value*.

Over the years eminent domain cases became my bread and butter because these cases are more likely than any other real estate transactions to lead the parties to the courthouse. Usually, the subject of the dispute is money. There are very few circumstances wherein the government can be made to give the property back. Most of the time (former) property owners don't believe that they have been paid "just and adequate compensation," and they almost always have a right to go to court.

The agency that "took" (condemning agencies almost always prefer the word "acquired") the property has the burden to prove that it has paid just and adequate compensation. It is the unusual property types, such as lands that contain proven reserves of merchantable minerals or "unique" properties, such as the last legal liquor store adjacent to a dry county, that are most likely to go to court.

Often the biggest dollar differences are associated with the property owner's claim of damages to the remaining property, not the value of the part taken. As so many of the appraisals I discuss in this book are associated with eminent domain cases, I will write much more about the process later.

Inverse Takings

Sometimes the government doesn't take your property, but it does something in your neighborhood that damages the value of your property. An example of one type of inverse condemnation would be airplane noise affecting the neighborhoods near the airport if the government does not condemn an avigation easement. Another might be a city building, landfill, or transfer station in your neighborhood, or closing a road that you needed to conduct your business. Life is much easier for an affected property owner when the government actually takes some of your property. Under a direct condemnation the taking entity has the obligation to prove that the amount of money that they offer constitutes "just and adequate" compensation. The burden of proof is on the government. In inverse condemnation proceedings the burden of proof shifts to the property owner, which is a much more difficult position to be in. You not only have to prove that some action taken near, but not on, your property caused you damage, but you also have to prove that the amount of your claim for damages is reasonable and actual, not speculative.

An inverse condemnation action is a cause of action by a citizen against a governmental defendant to recover the value of property that has been taken in fact, although no formal exercise of the power of eminent domain has been attempted by the taking agency.[11] Larry Smith, who is the Deputy County Attorney in Volusia County, Florida, supervising the litigation section of that office and lead trial attorney

---

[11] Florida Eminent Domain Practice and Procedure, Seventh Edition, The Florida Bar, 2008, section 13.2, page 13-2.

during numerous inverse condemnation cases involving flooding claims and Devo Seereeram, Ph.D., P.E., who is the Principal Engineer and owner of Devo Engineering, LLC located in Orlando, Florida, wrote a fine article on inverse condemnation associated with flooding "caused" by road construction.[12] This article, published on-line, discusses the engineer's point of view and the attorney's point of view in these types of cases.

I was involved with a series of inverse condemnation cases involving airplane noise. Almost two thousand homeowners in Virginia Beach, Virginia, contended that the Navy had damaged their homes by increasing the ambient noise at their location. There was no doubt that the Navy caused a substantial increase in noise by moving in the additional training flights. The entirety of that case was "proving" that the increase in noise did or did not damage property values.

Often "proving" that the public entity's action "caused" the problem is as troublesome and expensive as identifying and measuring the dollar amount of the damage. We, the people, are quick to form opinions, especially when we believe that we have been damaged. We tend to believe that we have been damaged, when in fact we may not have been damaged at all. I won't know that the value of my house has gone down until I try to sell it. If I find that it doesn't sell for as much as I thought it should, that may be because I haven't painted it in several years or because I painted it purple last year and not because the government put a half-way house for drug offenders on the next-door property.

---

[12] http://www.devoeng.com/memos/academia/inverse_condemnation_article_with_photos_with_endnotes.pdf.

Chapter 13: Tiananmen Square: Or What To Do When the Bulldozer Is at Your Door

I thought it might be useful to include a chapter of advice for the property owner who finds himself or herself in the path of progress. How can you best protect yourself when the city wants to widen the road in front of your house or the sewer company wants to build a lift station along the creek in your backyard? While I have never been charged with acquiring rights-of-way for a condemning agency, these observations and ideas are based on the hundreds of condemnations for which I have been an appraiser or an expert witness. Most of the time the condemnee, that is the person whose property is to be acquired, is facing the situation for the first time.

Eminent domain cases fall into two categories, the small money cases and the big money cases. The best strategy for the condemnee is similar in both cases, which is to get the best outcome at the lowest cost, but I think it is easier for me to talk about them in two parts.

In either situation, big money case or small, I think that the first step is to get a reasonable estimate of the extent to which the proposed governmental project is going to damage your property and/or your business. If you think that there is likely to be more than a few thousand dollars associated with the part taken and damage to your remainder property, I suggest that you go to the state Bar webpage in your state and look for attorneys in the eminent domain section. If your Bar doesn't have an eminent domain section, look for "condemnation" or "eminent domain" as filters for the attorney's areas of practice. Eminent domain is a narrowly focused area of practice and not something in which most attorneys are likely to have much experience. If you are facing hundreds of thousands of dollars in potential loss, you will want to find someone who is already an expert, not help create one.

When you interview attorneys you may retain for your case, try to learn the extent to which they work for the condemning authorities and the extent to which they work for the condemnees. Some work primarily for condemning authorities, like the Department of Transportation, while others, like my dear friend Richard Hubert, Esq., have never met a condemning authority they have liked. Richard will tilt at any windmill on the behalf of the property owner, come what may. In smaller or more rural communities it will be difficult to find an attorney who doesn't sometimes work for the local city or county or the DOT, but you will want to find someone who also has experience representing property owners subject to condemnation proceedings. The most important variable is to find someone you believe will represent you well and with whom you feel confident.

The Larger Money Cases

Any sizable condemnation case will require experts in addition to the attorney, among whom may be appraisers, land use planners, engineers, architects, traffic engineers, costing experts and anyone else who charges hundreds of dollars an hour and is necessary to make your case. With very few exceptions you will eventually have to hire at least an appraiser, but retain the attorney first. Ethical appraisers (and all the other professionals you may need) will provide their clients with the correct answer—to the best of their ability—when they are acting in their professional capacity. However, when and if they are in court as an expert witness, their real job is to be believed! Your attorney will be the best judge of the extent to which their experts are believable.

I mentioned "hundreds of dollars an hour" on purpose. My rates, when I retired from active practice, were $350/hour. In retirement I have raised my rates to $400/hour, and often I am the least well-paid person in the courtroom. I know, this sounds like the old joke about the two grocers on opposite corners. A customer at one was complaining about the price of bananas. She said: *$0.89/lb? Beckman's across the* street has bananas for $0.79/lb! Well, said the grocer, why didn't you buy them from Beckman's? The lady replied, He was out of bananas. Hell, said the grocer, when I am out of bananas they are only $0.69/lb! The sad truth is that there are relatively few appraisers who like to go to court. Most just don't like being cross-examined by a competent, well-paid advocate who is trying to make them look like a fool or a crook.

In Georgia and many other states, a person subject to eminent domain condemnation is entitled to just and adequate compensation **LESS THE COST OF GETTING IT!** In a few states, like Florida, the condemning authority pays for the property owner's attorney and experts in addition to their own. However, most states just hang their property owners out to dry. The reason is that in most states the legislature is a lot closer to the Power Company and the Highway Department and the other agencies most often involved as condemning authorities. Condemnees are affected one at a time and are seldom organized well enough or obtain enough public attention to have influence over the legislature. Also, the legislature wants as many miles of asphalt as possible from its highway budget, and any dollar paid to a property owner's lawyer or appraiser seems like a dollar wasted.

In many states the attorneys will accept contingent fees (usually plus a retainer), but that means that the attorney will take 30% to 40% of the eventual award above the original offer. It is not unusual for the appraiser and other experts to bill $20,000 or more, once one counts time for trial preparation, depositions and court. One can see that the costs to the property owner to contest an award by a condemning authority can mount up quickly. You must have a big enough difference of opinion about just and adequate compensation on the table before the fight becomes worthwhile.

If I am hired by an attorney, I don't offer any advice and I don't talk to the property owner unless I am in the presence of the attorney. I want to be certain that anything I say is privileged, and that I can't be forced to reveal any of my opinions that may hurt the property owner's case. I know that if I can't help, the attorney will fire me and look for someone else who might be more useful. After all, an appraisal is only an opinion.

I often advise property owners who have contacted me directly, without having found an attorney first, that unless there is more than $300,000 difference of opinion between the taking agency and the property owner they should find some way to settle without going to court. After all, if everyone does their job well, the highest probability is that the jury (or Trier of Fact) will split the baby down the middle, so the most likely award is $150,000 higher than the original offer. The attorney is likely to take a third, so we are now down to $100,000. The appraiser and other experts are likely to have cost $30,000 or $40,000, so the final difference is down to $60,000 or $70,000.

Now, $60,000 or $70,000 more than one started with sounds like a reasonably large amount of money, but the property owner has not yet accounted for the hundreds of man-hours that he may have to spend associated with the case. Neither does he account for the long time that may be involved between the time that the offer was first made and the date by which the money shows up. I have been involved in cases that have gone on for seven years. Condemning authorities may have to pay statutory interest on the award dating from the date of the take, but it still may not compensate the property owner sufficiently for his time and effort.

Usually the condemning authority's agents have some discretion in the amount that they can offer above the value determined by their appraisers. Often, when there is a big difference of opinion about just and adequate compensation between the taking agency and the property owner, the taking agency's offer would itself be a pretty big number. Say the original offer was about $700,000. A 10% increase in the negotiations would be as much as the $70,000 the property owner would be most likely to net from winning a $150,000 increase at a trial.

Honest appraisers will tell you that they would be happy if their single point estimate was within +/- 10%, so the taking agency's agents starting at $700,000 would be more likely than not to offer $770,000 or $800,000 just to make the situation go away. The acquisition agent's goal is to acquire all the required property in a timely fashion to permit the construction of the project. Condemnation is a tool within their toolbox, but it takes time and costs the agency money. If they could acquire the property by negotiation, they would prefer to. With all that said, if there is more than $300,000 difference of opinion between the parties, the best bet is to prepare for court and hope for the best when saner heads may prevail down the road.

Why Are There Likely To Be Big Differences between the Condemning Authority and the Property Owner?

In my experience, big differences come about from differences in judgments about the highest and best use of the property before and after the taking. In a later section of this book I talk about the case of a Ritz Camera Store. The business appraiser on the other side (representing the DOT) said that the business was worth nothing because silver film business was being taken over by digital photography. This was in spite of the fact that as of the date of taking, the store was still generating tens of millions of dollars in sales and throwing off hundreds of thousands of dollars in profits. $0 was the least believable number, even though two years later the whole national Ritz Camera chain was in bankruptcy.

Usually the biggest differences come about because the parties (and their appraisers) see the highest and best use of the remaining property after the taking very differently. I have often been in cases wherein all the parties saw the highest and best use of the property before the take the same way, and even saw the value variables the same way. The big difference wasn't associated with the value of the part taken by the condemnation. The big difference came about because after the taking the remainder property couldn't be used for the same purposes that it could before the taking. Sometimes the remainder property is now too small to support the type of development originally intended. Sometimes the acquisition removed a driveway or other access needed for the proposed development.

I recently heard a case where the power company took an easement that would permit them to run guy wires to high transmission poles anywhere they wished across the remainder property, making any development of the remainder problematic. If the condemnor's appraiser sees the remainder as $200/square foot land suitable for a high-rise, multiuse building (as it was before the taking) and the condemnee's appraiser sees the highest and best use of remainder as $60/square foot low-rise, apartment land there is going to be a big difference in the opinion of the value of the remainder following the taking. Neither appraiser really knows what the remainder property is going to be used for following the taking. It is only an opinion based on the differences in how they see the future for the property.

The condemning authority is obligated to pay not only the market value of the part taken, but any damages to the remainder after the take. Suppose both the condemnor's appraiser and the condemnee's appraiser saw the value of the property before the take as a relatively high value, say $200/square foot. After the take the condemnor's appraiser believed that there would be no change in highest and best use, whereas the condemnee's appraiser saw the value after the take at only $60/square foot, based on a change in highest and best use. In the opinion of the condemnee's appraiser the property was damaged by the loss of $140/square foot in value. Suppose there was about 20,000 square feet in the part taken, but there was an acre [43,560 square feet] in the remainder after the take. If the condemnor's appraiser said that there was no change from $200/square foot in the value of the remainder after the take and the condemnee's appraiser said that there was $140/square foot diminution in the value of the remainder after the take, the appraisal opinions of just and adequate compensation would differ by about $6,100,000 [43,560 * $140 = $6,098,400].

The Smaller Money Cases

Most of the time there is no big money on the table. Most condemnations involve a home owner or other small property owner and the taking is an unexpected disruption of one's life. It comes about when the highway department sends you a note that they plan to widen the road in front of your house, straighten out a curve, and take 40 feet off the frontage of your landscaped lot. Before the take the road was 100' from your front door and a huge Loropetalum hedge blocked the view of the traffic. After the take the road will pass 60' in front of your door and there will be no screen for the traffic.

Let's assume another few facts, just to illustrate the way that an appraiser might see the value issues. Most of your neighbors' houses were on ½-acre lots that were 100' wide by 200' deep and the houses were set back about 60' from the road. At least three vacant, ½-acre lots in your neighborhood recently sold for $20,000/lot or $1/sf for new houses. Before the taking, your lot was a little bigger than most because of the curve in the road. You used the extra space in your front yard for a lovely garden and, given the privacy that the hedge afforded you, you put in a bay window in the front of your house to bring the outside into your living room. After the take you will have lost the privacy and the hedge, if replanted, will take at least six years to grow big enough to replace the privacy.

You think that the new road project will ruin your property. No more garden area, no more privacy, no more need for the bay window. Living in your house will not be anywhere near as enjoyable after the take as it was before the take. After the take you think that your house is worthless, and that the city should buy the whole thing and you will leave! However, the appraiser for the highway department only wants the city to pay $1/sf or $4,000 for the land taken. After you engage in many frustrating phone calls, the city agrees to increase their offer by $800 to pay for the bushes.

The appraiser is charged with valuing market value, which means the value to the whole theoretical market of potential buyers. Sales of houses like yours throughout your subdivision all sell for roughly the same price without any measurable regard for front yard landscaping or privacy. Most are set back 60' from the road, just as yours will be following the taking. After the take your lot will be about as big as most of the lots in your subdivision. The appraiser can't find any measurable damage to your remainder property following the taking. The appraiser has sufficient evidence to support a value of $1/sf for the land.

You, on the other hand, have no interest in market value. You had no intention to sell. You liked your house as it was. You are only interested in the value of your property to you and your lifestyle. I think you will have a very hard time getting the appraiser or the courts to agree that your property has been made worthless. At the best, you may be able to claim that your bay window is now functionally obsolete, but I doubt that you will be successful with even this claim. In my case study, the market just doesn't recognize an increment of value for the extra privacy and the extra acreage in the front yard.

I very recently had a call from a retired fellow in a neighboring suburban community. The three former minifarms that formed the three sides of his parcel were all being developed with subdivisions. He and his wife ran a horse farm on a 5-acre tract that was one of the few remaining semirural tracts in a rapidly urbanizing area. They gave riding lessons and stabled and pastured horses and offered trail rides, which provided them a lovely home and a very satisfactory retirement income of about $40,000/year, net of all expenses.

The neighboring city's gas department was running a new gas main along the frontage road, and the fellow had learned that the gas line was going to come inside his fence and cut a swath along the frontage of his property, taking down the trees that provided a substantial degree of privacy and taking down the fence that kept the horses inside that front pasture.

Often cities or counties, schools, and the utilities that have been empowered to use eminent domain only occasionally undertake projects that may require them to condemn properties. Unlike the state highway department or the major power companies, they are not used to using eminent domain and may not cross all the 'T's or dot all the 'I's. As of the time he called me, this fellow had not been contacted by the city. He had not given anyone permission to put a new gas pipe along the frontage of his property. Everything he knew had come from articles in the local newspaper and a conversation with the bulldozer operator who was working on properties less than a mile down the road from his property. He had called a lawyer whom he knew, who happened to be one of our state's better-known eminent domain specialists, and he was advised to call me, which he did.

He called me for an appraisal, but I explained that I was unreasonably expensive, and—if he determined that he had to have professional help—that I would probably turn out to be the least expensive part of his team. He seemed a capable enough person over the phone, and I advised him to try to handle the problem himself.

I told him that it was very unlikely that he could do anything about the project or how it was going to affect his property. At this stage of the game the whole issue was about money, and that if he thought that he could keep his emotions out of the picture, he would probably not have to hire an attorney to keep from having a heart attack or a stroke. He was already past the annoyance of having his life disrupted and had accepted the inevitability of the project, but he wanted to be sure that he was being treated fairly.

As the city planned only to acquire an easement in which to bury the new gas line, I advised him that they would not pay very much money for the easement. Easements very seldom sell on the open market, so the appraiser must first find evidence of the market value of similar land in fee simple, and then make a judgment about the share of the fee simple value that goes with the easement and the part that remains with the (former) fee owner, now subordinate to the easement. Even if land in that area is reasonably expensive, say $100,000/acre as subdivision land instead of $20,000/acre as farm land, the take only affects a swath 20' wide by 500' long or 10,000 square feet of land, or 0.23/acre or $23,000 in fee simple. Say the appraiser values the easement at 50% of the fee simple value. The offer for the easement will be only about $11,500.

The 10,000 square feet of land in the permanent easement is only a part of the story. During the period of construction, the contractor must have more room to maneuver, so the city acquires a temporary easement 10' wide on either side of the permanent easement. This is an additional 10,000 sf of land affected. As we discussed earlier, the appraiser must estimate the rent-use price for the land in the temporary easement for the duration of the construction period. The easement documents, when finally drawn and presented to the landowner, indicate a three-year construction period. Our state law requires that there be a stated construction period, but many times smaller jurisdictions or occasional condemning authorities don't pay a lot of attention to construction easements. Assume in this example that the city has the documents but figured that they would only need a month at the most to lay the pipe across this fellow's horse farm, so their offer for the temporary easement was a nominal $500.

The owner, on the other hand, believed that if the temporary easement stated three years, he should be paid for the rent of his 10,000 square feet of land at 10% of the market value, or $2.33/sf time 3 or $2,330/year, for a total of $6,990. However, having read my arguments about having to calculate the present value of the cash flow for a temporary easement, he estimated a 10% discount rate or $5,794, rounded to $5,800 to cover the three years in the temporary easement.

I told him that his first step was to make a list of the ways that the taking was going to affect him and to put dollar signs associated with each component. The project was going to require the demolition of the fencing along a part of the sidelines of his pasture and all the frontage, so the contractor could bring in the heavy equipment required for the project. Consequently, during the construction period he would have to construct temporary fencing to protect the horses in the front pasture. He was getting bids from a couple of contractors for the temporary fencing and for the cost of the permanent fencing following the completion of the project. The contractor had said that the city would replace the permanent fencing as a part of the project, but the property owner needed to know how much that would cost in case the city's budget was unreasonably low. For purposes of my example, let's say that a couple of independent contractors quoted $3,500 for the temporary fencing and $12,500 to replace the permanent fencing. The city estimated that it would cost them $8,000 to replace the permanent fencing.

The fellow had built new fencing on that frontage two years ago at a cost of $12,000, and the fence was supposed to last 10 years. Even assuming it was 20% depreciated, it had a remaining contributory value of $9,600, and the city was going to take the fencing. The $9,600 should be considered as a part of the take, whereas the $12,500 or $8,000 to rebuild the fence after the project is finished is a part of the cost-to-cure. Another part of the cost-to-cure is the $2,200 estimate for reseeding the swath of the pasture in the temporary easement and the permanent easement following the construction.

The project was going to require the removal of a copse of trees that had grown naturally along the frontage of the fellow's property, outside of the street right-of-way. These trees belonged to the property owner, but since they were naturally growing pines, the city wouldn't consider that they were planted landscaping and wouldn't compensate the owner. I suggested that he contact a registered forester to estimate the board feet of merchantable timber in that copse. The city's contract for the removal of the trees may have recognized an offset for the sale of the timber, but the money for the timber should have gone to the owner of the trees, not to the benefit of the condemning authority. In this example assume that the forester estimated the timber value at $3,500.

During the period of the construction the fellow will have to increase the amount of stall feeding for the horses boarded at his farm because of both the reduction in the size of his front pasture and the noise of the construction. He estimated that he would have to hire half-time temporary help for at least six weeks at $15/hour and increase his silage bill by $3,000 until the grass regrew in the pasture.

In this example I estimated the property owner's estimate of the cost of the condemnation and the city's estimate:

LOWER VALUE EMINENT DOMAIN EXAMPLE

ITEM	ESTIMATE	OFFER
REAL ESTATE RELATED		
Take-Permanent Easement	$12,650	$11,500
Take - Temporary Easement	$5,800	$500
Timber	$3,500	$0
Permanent Fencing	$9,600	$0
Cost to Cure - Fencing	$12,500	$8,000
Cost to Cure - Reseeding	$2,200	$0
SUBTOTAL, REAL ESTATE TAKEN	$46,250	$20,000
BUSINESS RELATED		
Temporary Fencing	$3,500	$0
Temporary Labor	$1,800	$0
Additional Silage	$3,000	$0
SUBTOTAL - BUSINESS RELATED	$8,300	$0
TOTAL COMPENSATION	$54,550	$20,000
DIFFERENCE	$34,550	

In this case, the property owner believes that he should be paid $54,550 and the city's offer is $20,000. This $34,550 difference is not worth a court fight, but certainly is worth the owner's time in trying to negotiate.

In this case, $26,250 of the difference of opinion is associated with the real estate, and should not be too hard to settle, because the city knows it must pay just and adequate compensation for the real estate taken. The other $8,300 is really associated with the horse farm's business. Given the parameters we have presented with the horse farm generating $40,000 net income after all expenses, it probably has a market value as a business of $200,000 using a 20% cap rate (or 5X multiple of earnings). The business can't operate without the temporary fencing or the additional labor and silage. If the issue were to go to condemnation in Georgia, Florida or another state that recognized business damages, the owner would claim loss of the $200,000 business if there were no $8,300 cost-to-cure, which might increase the chances that the city would negotiate rather than condemn. However, if this was a Federal taking or a taking in a state that used the federal rule, the owner would be out of luck for that $8,300 part of his damages.

The most important point for the owner to realize is that he only gets one bite at the apple, and it happens before, not after, the project. If the owner has the right to prevent the bulldozer from coming on his property he is in the strongest bargaining position he can be in. The contractor is already on the street and the city will want to obtain the right for him to continue the project as soon as possible. The contractor will get paid for delays and the city wants the project completed.

Make no mistake, if the owner is being stubborn and the city has its documents prepared, condemnation can happen in a moment. Once the property is condemned the title transfers to the condemning authority, and any dispute is a legal matter that will require an attorney. Consequently, the property owner's least-cost course of action is to negotiate, and to negotiate he must be prepared. In this case, if the horse farm owner followed my advice, he would be well prepared, and all the dollar estimates associated with his claim for compensation would be documented by third-party bids. Just think how much better off he will be if he can get half of the difference between the original offer and his estimate.

Chapter 14: I Know What the Whole Thing's Worth. What Is My Part Worth?

Limited partnerships (LPs), family limited partnerships (FLPs), limited liability companies (LLCs), real estate investment trusts (REITS) and other special interest pass-through entities are tools by which folks convert the ownership of the whole thing into pieces. These entities are called "pass-through entities" because the income or losses associated with the entity are passed through to the owners of the fractional interests on a pro rata basis. Any tax consequence associated with the income or loss is reflected on the fractional owner's personal income tax return.

Sometimes investors know from the beginning that fractional interests will be the type of ownership that makes the investment possible, as is the case with REITS. After all, there are a lot more people who can invest $1,000 each to buy a $10,000,000 property than there are people who can buy a $10,000,000 property. In other cases, Papa wants to preserve the integrity of his investment portfolio despite his concern about the incompetence of his heirs, but he knows that he won't live forever, and he wants to begin to transfer his wealth to his incompetent progeny without having it lost to drugs, gambling and divorce.

At the same time there is an essential difference between owning the whole megillah, which means owning something in fee simple, and owning a fractional interest. When you own a fractional interest, like owning a share of stock in a publicly traded company, you own an intangible. Nowadays when you own a share of stock you seldom even get the engraved piece of paper.

Furthermore, the market knows that the value of the whole is worth more than the sum of its parts. Most of the time when a publicly traded company purchases a controlling interest in another publicly traded company it pays a premium over the total value of invested capital (trading price of a share in the acquired company multiplied by the total number of outstanding shares).

What are these acquiring companies paying for when they pay more for the whole than they would have to pay for all the shares? Sometimes they think that they are buying a synergy that will make both companies worth more together than either was by itself. Sometimes they are trying to buy an idea or a brand or people that they think will give them a boost. However, always they are buying control and control always costs more than a minority fractional interest.

Just think for a minute about what you get when you have control. You get to be the decider. You can select management and hire and fire staff. You decide on the capital structure, what part equity and what part debt. You decide what to do about product and process. You decide on to whom to rent and at what price. You decide when to sell.

Fractional Interests Discounts for Lack of Control

The other side of a premium for control is a discount for a lack of control, which is why a 20% interest in a family limited partnership is worth something less than 20% of the underlying assets owned by the partnership.

One of my favorite passages in the IRS Regulations states: *In valuing partial interests the burden of proof of the amount of the discount (from the proportional share of the underlying asset) is on the taxpayer, **and the only effective evidence of a discount is the testimony of a competent appraiser.***[13] That statement earned me a lot of money. Usually, when someone creates an FLP or LLC or tenancy-in-common

---

[13] See Tax Coordinator, p-6150, 6151.

(TIC) they are mindful of the tax consequence of creating a fractional interest.

The IRS will ignore any of these pass-through entities unless the parties can prove that the entity was created for a legitimate business purpose, not just as a device to avoid taxes. Fortunately, there are many legitimate business reasons that give rise to a need to create a fractional ownership interest. Affordability, the need to preserve a pool of assets and the need to distribute shares in those assets are but a few of the legitimate business reasons I have seen in my practice.

Under current Federal income tax regulations, gifts of $15,000 to a single individual do not give rise to a gift tax either to the donor or the recipient. Suppose Grandpa had a pool of assets that were worth $30,000,000 and he wanted to begin to pass these assets on to his eventual heirs and reduce the eventual estate tax at his death. At the same time, he wanted to preserve the underlying assets from the exigencies of accident and divorce and other perils of our foolish, human lives. He could establish an FLP and transfer the assets to the FLP. He could remain the general partner (or assign that function to another) by transferring as little as 1% to the general partner. He would then own a 99% limited partnership interest in the underlying pool.

The limited partnership rights are determined by the partnership agreement. If he were to be divorced in a community property state, or if he were to be sued, the assets he now owns are the intangible family limited partnership interests, not the underlying pool of assets. A successful plaintiff or his ex can only get to the FLP interests, not a pro rata share of the underlying $30,000,000. This is the case even if the $30,000,000 was cash or marketable securities.

Most of these FLP agreements severely limit the rights of transferees or assignees. A transferee or assignee does not automatically attain the status of a limited partner. Often the transferee has no right to see the books, attend meetings, vote or convert their assignee status into a limited partnership without the approval of the general partner and the other limited partners. The other partners probably will have right of first refusal to match any bona fide offer to purchase the assignee's interest, and the assignee may be forced to take payment at a nominal interest rate over an extended period. State laws exist to protect both limited partners and assignees from outrageously onerous constraints, but a limited partner's position is truly limited, and the position of an assignee is even further limited.

Only the general partner can control the partnership's assets. That means that even if the assets generate income, even a substantial income, the general partner decides how much of that income will be distributed to the partners. Each limited partner will get his or her pro rata share of any income that is distributed, but 20% of $0 is still $0.

The evidence of the amount of a discount that the market extracts for the lack of control associated with a limited partnership unit in an FLP is the opinion of a qualified appraiser, but the appraiser must base his opinion on generally accepted methods and facts.

Suppose, for example, the $30,000,000 asset that had been placed in an FLP was a well-established funeral home. Suppose, further, you owned 20% of the FLP. The pro rata value of your share would be $6,000,000. Suppose further that several competing national chains had been buying up funeral homes like yours and had been paying $1.30 for every $1.00 of value. Suppose even further that the FLP had several offers to purchase the funeral home for about $30,000,000. Under that set of circumstances, it would be reasonable for the appraiser to conclude that the premium for control was about 50% ($15,000,000 premium on a $30,000,000 base value).

With that information in hand, the appraiser could conclude that the market extracted a 33% discount for lack of control. Certainly, if the partnership were to sell for $45,000,000, you would be entitled to $9,000,000, or a 50% premium. However, if Grandpa, who was still the general partner, turned down the offer, you couldn't do anything about it. You couldn't even get to your $6,000,000 pro rata share. The reciprocal of a 50% premium is a 33% discount ($1/1.5 = 0.66667$; $1 - 0.66667 = 0.33333$ or 33%). Consequently, it would be reasonable for the appraiser to conclude that the market value of your $6,000,000 pro rata share wouldn't be worth any more than $4,020,000 reflecting a 33% discount for lack of control.

Discounts for Lack of Marketability

Discounts for lack of control are not the only discounts that the market extracts. One must also consider the marketability of the asset being appraised as compared to assets that are freely traded on an open market. As we discussed earlier in this book, marketability for an intangible asset generally means nominal marketing costs and cash within three days, based on the public stock markets. If the transaction costs are more than a few tenths of a percent and the time to get the cash is more than three days, the market imposes a discount.

Suppose you own the 20% limited partnership share in the Wise Funeral Home and you want to cash out. Where will you go to find your buyer? Wise Funeral FLP isn't listed on any stock exchange. Coldwell Banker Real Estate Brokers won't be any help. A business broker may take on the assignment, but the business broker's commission will be north of 10% plus expenses, and according to Tom West's "Business Reference Guide," fewer than 20% of small, privately held businesses listed for sale ever sell. Selling a 20% interest in an FLP is less attractive than a controlling interest in a small business. Marketing this asset is likely to require a substantial discount.

One of the things an appraiser may do to estimate an appropriate discount for marketability would be to interview business brokers to ask their opinion about the magnitude of discount they thought would be required to sell the asset. When all else fails, opinion evidence is better than nothing. After all, opinion evidence is how I made my living.

Another slightly more persuasive method the appraiser may have tried would be to make some estimate of the time that it may take to market something like a $6,000,000 interest in an FLP. Say he gets evidence that it will take a year to liquidate the asset and that given the regular cash flow to the FLP, a supportable risk rate for this asset is 20%.

That means that the present value of the asset recognizing the year's delay is a discount of 20% plus another 10% transaction fee, and then a 30% discount to make this asset as marketable as a share of a publicly traded stock.

Several United States Tax Court cases deal directly with a discount for lack of control associated with a minority interest, discounts for the difficulties in marketing a minority interest (illiquidity and marketability), and discounts for a lack of diversity in the underlying asset. The cases point out that the discount for one type of problem should be added to the discount for another type of problem.[14]

If the appraiser was correct in assigning a 33% discount for lack of control and a 30% discount for lack of marketability, the market value of the 20% interest would be $3,186,000 based on an underlying pro rata value of $6,000,000, since the discounts are applied sequentially [$6,000,000*.67 = $4,020,000 * .7 = $2,814,000]. This represents a combined discount of 53% from the pro-rata value.

Think of the tax consequences associated with an appraisal that supported a total 53% discount for lack of control and lack of marketability. Assume that the FLP established 100,000 limited partnership units. Based on the $30,000,000 value of the underlying asset each unit would have a pro rata value of $300/unit. However, the market value would only be $140.70/unit. That means Grandpa could gift almost 106 units to each of his heirs and not exceed the $15,000 annual tax-exempt limit on a single gift. At $400/unit (pro rata value) Grandpa would be limited to gifting 37.5 units/year to each of his heirs. By creating the FLP Grandpa was able to annually distribute more than three times the ownership of Wise Funeral Home without tax. Assume Grandpa had three children and ten grandchildren. Each year he could gift 1,386 units of the FLP without anyone incurring any income tax

---

[14] Andrews v. Commissioner, 79 TC 938; Ward v. Commissioner, 87 TC 78; Piper v. Commissioner, 72 TC, 1062; Estate of Edgar A. Berg, Tax Court Reports, 2949-2959, and In re: Guido Frezzo, Debtor, No. 97-16286SR, WL 97425 (U.S. Bankruptcy Court, E.D. Pennsylvania, March 5, 1998, Judge Raslavich, and Williams v. Commissioner, No. 219-96, 220-96, 221-96, 1998 WL 55347 (United States Tax Court, February 12, 1998), Judge Colvin.

and without giving up any control of the Wise Funeral Home.

Furthermore, assume nothing changed in the value of the FLP over a 20-year horizon (which, I know, is an unrealistic assumption, but it makes the example less complicated). Assume that in 20 years Grandpa died. Over the years Grandpa would have gifted 27,719 units of the FLP reducing his ownership to 72,281 units. The pro rata value of his estate would be reduced to $21,684,435. However, the market value of his FLP units would only be worth $10,170,000. Since the first $10,170,000 of an estate is tax exempt as of the writing of this chapter, Grandpa would have reduced the taxable basis of his estate from $10,284,435 (assuming no FLP) to $0, part by gift and part associated with the FLP discount for lack of control and lack of marketability. Not a bad savings for the cost of a good tax planner, an estate attorney and a competent appraiser.

Tenancy in Common

Many people find themselves owning a fractional interest in real estate because they inherited property where there was no will. If I have three kids and I die without a will each of my kids will inherit a one-third undivided interest in what had been my property. If what I had was something that cannot easily be subdivided into equal parts to be distributed in fee simple, say the 100 acres containing a cave described in an earlier chapter, the beneficiaries of my estate wind up owning something together. This type of ownership is called tenancy in common (TIC) or undivided interests (UDI).

TICs or UDIs impose the same kind of trouble for appraisers that are associated with FLPs or LLCs or other fractional interests. It isn't hard to decide on the value of the entirety of the underlying property, but the appraisal of the appropriate discounts for lack of control and lack of marketability becomes a problem. The professional journal of the Institute of Business Appraisers, *Business Appraisal Practice*, published an article on the solution to the fractional interest problem I wrote for those of you who want some more detail on this type of appraisal.[15]

Publicly Registered but Privately Traded Limited Partnerships

One of the best analogues to a family limited partnership or to a tenancy-in-common is the marketplace made up of trades in publicly registered but privately traded limited partnerships. The limited partners do not have any control over the underlying assets. There is a market made up of about a dozen brokers, but there is nothing equivalent to the public markets wherein an investor can execute a trade and receive cash in three days with very little transaction cost. The partnership market imposes substantial costs of sale and usually results in cash in six to eight weeks. These publicly registered partnerships are still superior to a family limited partnership or a private tenancy-in-common because any potential investor can review the financial reports (10K and 10Q reports) filed with the SEC, whereas there generally is no right to information associated with the private fractional interests we are asked to appraise.

Spencer Jefferies has reported on this market for years, providing detailed information on trades and the discounts from the pro rata share of the underlying assets in *Partnership Spectrum* and related periodicals and books.[16] Mr. Jefferies's materials make it possible to match asset characteristics, such as the mix of equity and debt, the history of distributions and the character of the underlying pool of assets. He also reports the number of transactions, the number of units traded in any transaction and the value of the pro rata share of the underlying assets. He reports the source of the value estimates, whether made by the general partner or by an independent appraiser.

The data is carefully maintained and covers a multiyear history,

---

[15] "Valuing a Tenancy-In-Common," Henry J. Wise, MAI, CBA, BVAL, CRE; Published in *Business Appraisal Practice*, Journal of the Institute of Business Appraisers, Fall 2003, pp. 4-18.

[16] See also, COMPREHENSIVE GUIDE FOR THE VALUATION OF FAMILY LIMITED PARTNERSHIPS, Second Edition, 2003. Bruce A. Johnson, Spencer Jefferies, James A. Park, Partnership Profiles, Inc.

making it possible for the appraiser to view changes in the marketplace over time. Students of the *Partnership Spectrum* survey of discounts point out that the discounts reflect both a discount for lack of control (DLOC) and a discount for lack of marketability (DLOM). However, as Spencer Jefferies reports in the May/June 2003 issue of *Partnership Spectrum*, most of the discount must be associated with the DLOC, because there is an active and organized market for publicly registered and privately traded limited partnership units.

At least a dozen reasonably well-advertised firms make a market in these units, and sellers can effect a sale within a few days and get paid generally within 60 days. Certainly, there is a discount required for the time value of money over a 60-day window as compared to a three-day window for publicly traded stocks, but that increment of discount is probably very small, and probably one could measure the increment by comparing the overnight funds rates to a 60- or 90-day certificate of deposit at the local bank.[17]

The IRS hates pass-through entities and one can easily understand why. Throughout all the years Grandpa still controlled Wise Funeral Home and kept most of the benefits of ownership. The Service's argument is usually based on the idea that wrapping Wise Funeral Home in a piece of paper really changed nothing. If it was worth $20,000,000 the day before the FLP it couldn't have lost $12,600,000 or 63% of its value overnight. However, it is the market that imposes discounts for lack of control and lack of marketability, not the appraiser. One might just as well ask how it is possible for a brand-new car to lose 15% of its value just by being driven from the showroom to my garage.

Much depends on the appraiser in valuing these pass-through entities and the appraiser has very limited data about very fuzzy markets upon which to base his opinions. Furthermore, because there is so much difference in tax liability between the value of the underlying asset within the pass-through entity and outside it, the IRS imposes substantial penalties on appraisers that they believe do not have a

---

[17] The Partnership Spectrum, May/June 2003, page 9.

reasonable foundation for their opinion.[18]

Sales of Undivided Interests

As a part of a nationwide search I undertook for actual sales of real estate based partial interests, Mary G. Gates, an appraiser at Arthur Gimmy International of San Francisco, California, sent information on three sales that took place between 1987 and 1990. I have been unable to obtain independent confirmations of the facts of these transactions but believe that the following descriptions of the facts are reliable.

Sale No. 1 was the 1988 sale of a 25% undivided interest in the Sobel Building at 680 8th Street, San Francisco, California. The 87,404 sf, one- and two-story showroom/mart building had been independently appraised at $8,000,000. The building was leased to a third-party tenant for a term of 25 years, with a nine-year option. The Grantor had originally purchased the property in 1956 as a tenant-in-common with two others. One of these fractional owners tried unsuccessfully to market his 25% interest to third parties before he sold to the remaining partners for $1,256,000, or a 37% discount from a 25% pro rata share of the appraised fee simple value.

Sale No. 2 is the February 1990 sale of a 50% undivided interest in the leased fee of a long-term ground lease under a market in Antioch,

---

[18] 20.1.12.1 (08-27-2010) Overview

The Service has authority to penalize and to seek injunctions against appraisers. Prior to the passage of the Pension Protection Act of 2006 (Pub. L. No. 109-280), appraisers could only be subject to penalties under IRC 6700, Promoting abusive tax shelters, etc., or IRC 6701, Penalties for aiding and abetting understatement of tax liability.

Section 1219 of the Pension Protection Act of 2006 added IRC 6695A, Substantial and Gross Valuation Misstatements Attributable to Incorrect Appraisals. This new penalty provision allows the Service to assert a penalty against any person who prepared an appraisal of the value of property and who knew, or reasonably should have known, the appraisal would be used in connection with a return or claim for refund and that appraisal results in a substantial valuation misstatement (within the meaning of IRC 6662(e)), a substantial estate or gift tax valuation understatement (within the meaning of IRC 6662(g)), or a gross valuation misstatement (within the meaning of IRC 6662(h)) with respect to such property.

The amount of the IRC 6695A penalty is the lesser of 10 percent of the amount of the underpayment (defined by IRC 6664(a)) attributable to the misstatement - or – $1,000,- or –125 percent of the gross income received from the preparation of the appraisal.

California. All parties agreed that the value of the leased fee at the time of the sale was $455,000, based on a lease to run for 46 years from the date of the sale. Prior to the sale, two unrelated families owned the leased fee. After trying unsuccessfully for a period to market the 50% interest to a third party, one family sold to the other family for $165,000, or a 27% discount from the value of the pro rata share.

Sale No. 3 reflects a discount of between 27% to 41% from the pro rata share of a 25% partnership in a 582-acre tract near Benecia, California, used for grazing cattle. The partners were an uncle and a nephew. The fee simple interest in the tract was appraised as being in a range of between $1,200/acre to $1,500/acre. The 25% share sold for $128,000 or a discount of 27% if the market value of the fee simple position was worth $1,200/acre or a discount of 41% if the market value of the fee simple position was worth $1,500/acre. The discounts for these three sales of undivided interests ranged from a low of 27% to a high of 41%.

On September 12, 2000, I interviewed F.W. "Fritz" Wellmann of Washington, Texas. Mr. Wellmann has made a market in undivided interest (UDI) acquisitions in his area, purchasing the fractions and reassembling the entire fee. According to Mr. Wellmann, the trouble is that after one gets into a UDI deal one often learns that there is a real problem in finding one or two of the heirs who own a fractional interest. Then one has either to partition the land, physically, or ask the court to order a public sale and partition the money obtained from the public sale.

Mr. Wellmann stated: *Because no one (no broker) handles this type of property you never pay dollar for dollar for the property. I never pay more than $0.50 on the dollar, and if it is a difficult case with numerous parties, I may pay only $0.33 on the dollar. You need the difference to pay attorney fees and other related costs to assemble the entirety. It often takes three years to reassemble all or enough of the parts to have a useful property.* Mr. Wellmann reported that he has one partition that has been in the works for 10 years.

The most illustrative finding from this review of the sales is that there is generally no third-party buyer (a buyer that is not already a part of the entity that owns the underlying asset). The sales of fractional interests are time-consuming, difficult and complicated transactions. Even the long-term co-owners are generally not willing to pay the pro rata share represented by a partial interest without demanding some discount. My study of this market convinces me that a partial interest is highly illiquid and has substantial problems of marketability.

Chapter 15: Senior Living

The older I get the more I think about the component of the real estate world that generally falls under the title of "senior living." This type of housing ranges all the way from subdivisions or apartment houses restricted to persons age 55 or older to Alzheimer wards in skilled nursing homes.

The residential properties that are most ubiquitous and constitute the lower end of the continuum are rental, independent-living apartment units that are age restricted. Further along the continuum are assisted-living units that require much larger service staffs and the total value must include some component of business value to account for the greater risks and the larger staff.

Continuing care retirement communities (CCRC), semiskilled nursing homes, skilled nursing homes and hospitals often are businesses that require a certificate of need (CON) from the state Health Planning Agency, a large, trained (and often state-certified and/or regulated) staff and a substantial capital investment in real estate to fulfill their essential purpose. As senior living facilities provide more and more services and the tenants are more and more dependent on their caregivers for safety, security, physical and mental health and the activities of daily living, the more they attract the attention of state regulatory agencies and the more business value they contain.

Most of us don't care about the extent to which "the old folks home" is classified as a business or as real estate, but most of us are not trying to underwrite real estate mortgage loans or trying to apply property taxes to real property and not to intangibles.

Mortgage lenders need to know the share of the total asset that is real estate as compared to personal property or intangible business value. The bank examiners treat these different classes of assets differently, so the banks are concerned. Unhappy property owners who believe that the tax assessors have substantially overvalued their senior living facility by including the business intangibles in their real estate assessment for property tax purposes are another group of people who care about this issue.

This isn't a big national issue because the owners of most senior living facilities are churches or fraternal organizations or other entities that are exempt from property taxes, but some of these facilities are owned by ordinary people or corporations that must pay their property taxes.

The taxes are generally limited to ad valorem taxes for the real estate and the personal property, not the intangibles. The appraiser's problem is one of separating the value of the whole into its component parts. Often the dollar amounts of the property taxes under dispute are not large enough to warrant the expense and risk of litigation. However, I had two cases wherein the property owners got mad enough and dollars involved were big enough to bring the issue to court.

Continuing Care Retirement Community (CCRC) Example

The case I liked the best, both because it was a big win and because it illustrates so many aspects about valuation, involved a CCRC in DeKalb County, Georgia. This was a "luxury cruise ship" of a CCRC. It had detached and attached houses for independent living, apartment-like assisted living units, a semiskilled nursing area, a skilled nursing area and an Alzheimer's ward. It even had a 50-bed acute care hospital on premises. There were three white linen, crystal and silver dining rooms, a great bar and lounge, indoor and outdoor swimming pools, a concierge, and a complete gym. The facility was located adjacent to a major park and a golf course, and the residents had direct access to these amenities.

There was a full-time staff of about 130 people required to serve the approximately 400 residents living in 300 dwelling units. Most of the detached houses and attached independent living units were occupied by couples, whereas most of the assisted-living and nursing-home units were single occupancy. The average age of the residents was 83.

Unit of Comparison

In the senior living trade there is a good deal of confusion engendered by the way we describe occupancy. Facilities that are most like conventional apartment houses generally describe themselves as having "x" number of units or apartments, and further break down the description by number of bedrooms and bathrooms per unit, i.e. 15 efficiency units; 25 one-bedroom units; 10 two-bedroom, one-bath units; 5 two-bedroom, two-bath units, etc. As facilities move towards the end of the spectrum wherein the residents require more services, they tend to describe themselves by number of beds, i.e. 60 assisted-living beds, 40 semiskilled nursing beds; 50 skilled nursing beds, 20 Alzheimer's beds, etc. Lower-priced facilities of this type may have as many as four beds and one bathroom per room, whereas higher-priced facilities are usually one bed and a private bath per room.

State Regulation Matters

The selection of how the facility describes itself usually begins with the extent to which the facility is regulated by the state. Independent living age restricted units usually do not fall under any state regulatory body, which means that any real estate developer can build wherever and whenever he wishes, hoping that there will be sufficient demand to make his development successful. As a part of the nation's attempt to control health care costs, nursing home and hospital beds require a "certificate of need" (CON) from the Regional Health Planning Agency (HPA). CONs become a license to build and operate, and the CON can have great value as an intangible asset independent of the real estate. Assisted living facilities fall somewhere in the middle, depending on the state.

The difficulty that this dichotomy of description (either units or beds) poses for the appraiser is in selecting an appropriate unit of comparison for the appraisal. Does one describe the subject based on the number of bedrooms or number of units or number of beds? The appraiser and the reader of the appraisal report can overcome this problem by documenting the unit of comparison and by being consistent in treating the comparable properties the same as one treats the subject property. In fact, being consistent is much harder to do than to say. A lot of inappropriate appraisal opinions and misunderstandings are associated with the appraiser's failure to select and consistently apply an appropriate unit of comparison when dealing with senior living facilities.

Impact of Property Tax Liability

In the case described above all the parties agreed that the CCRC that was the subject of my appraisal cost $46,000,000 to build. The first-year property taxes could be levied, the County tax assessors "did the owner a favor" by valuing the real estate at only $40,000,000. Property taxes in our urban areas generally amount to about 2% of the value of the real estate as estimated by the tax assessors, or an annual tax bill of $800,000 on a valuation of $40,000,000.

Although the property owners admitted that the facility cost $46,000,000 to build, things are not always worth what they cost, which is why the market uses an income approach and a sales comparison approach in addition to the cost approach to value assets. At a valuation of $40,000,000, each of the 300 units at the subject would have a contributory value of $133,333/unit. The highest value that the DeKalb County Tax Assessors had on the best apartments in the County was about $60,000/unit.

Across the Fence Alternative Valuation

If the County had treated the subject as if it were the most valuable apartment house in the County at $60,000/unit, the 300-unit development would have been valued at $18,000,000 and the property tax bill would have been about $360,000. The potential $440,000 difference in the annual property tax bill looked a lot bigger than the maximum likely cost to fund the case, so the attorneys and I were hired.

The income approach analysis cast much more suspicion on the County's valuation of $40,000,000. Within three months of obtaining its certificate of occupancy the facility was 81% occupied and generated an average rent of $2,100/month or a total income of about $6,125,000/year. The highest competitive rent in the County for a conventional apartment unit was about $1,200/month. The average $2,100/month at the subject was similar to the monthly charge at generally comparable assisted living facilities and private nursing homes nominally owned by churches or 501-c (3) tax exempt entities. "Rent" at the subject covered at least two meals per day, and for most of the residents it also included assistance in bathing and dressing, nursing services and other services required by the fragile elderly (often called activities of daily living or ADLs).

Operating expenses were relatively high, having to pay for a large 24-hour staff, food, and other consumable supplies. The net operating income (NOI) amounted to about $3,380,000, which, when capitalized at a 13% overall capitalization rate, indicated a value as a going concern at $26,000,000. A 13% overall capitalization rate was reasonably supported by the handful of generally similar CCRCs sold throughout the country as going concerns.

All the parties agreed that the personal property at the subject contributed about $2,000,000 to the overall value. The difficulty was in determining how much of the remaining $24,000,000 was associated with the real estate and how much was associated with the intangible business of running a CCRC.

Extracting Business Value from Value of the Going Concern

As a business appraiser I consulted the usual databases of private company transactions. The sales listed in the IBA database, Pratts Stats and Bizcomps indicated to me that the appropriate value metrics extracted from the market of sales of CCRC type businesses (NAICS code 62331), excluding tangible property, was about one times gross receipts and about five times EBIDTA (earnings before interest, depreciation, taxes and amortization). Both these statistics indicated that the value of the subject's intangible business was about $6,000,000. Consequently, the contributory value of the real estate excluding the personal property and the intangibles was about $18,000,000, or about $60,000/unit. At that valuation the property taxes would be about $360,000/year.

Fortunately for my client, Georgia law states that if a property owner has to go to Superior Court to appeal his taxes (which is going above the usual administrative procedure of appealing to the Board of Equalization), and if the taxpayer wins a tax assessment reduction of 20% or more, the County must pay the taxpayer's legal expenses. This case cost the County slightly over $140,000 to pay for the taxpayer's attorneys, me and the other witnesses[19].

How Can Something That Cost $46 Million To Build Be Worth $18 Million As Real Estate?

Most of you who have been willing to chew through this story to this point must be left with the burning question: How can a rational, economically motivated private businessman pay $46,000,000 to build an asset which, when occupied and operating, is worth no more than $26,000,000 as a going concern? The answer is in the financing that the developer employed. To move in when one wants to, one had first to buy a membership. Memberships cost from $225,000 to $350,000, depending on the type of housing one wanted. The member is guaranteed at least 90% of the purchase price of the membership returned when the member vacates the facility. Within the first three

[19] The case referenced in this article was in the Superior Court of DeKalb County, State of Georgia; Civil Action File Number 05cv9893-1; Parkside at Stone Mountain, LLC, FKA Stone Mountain, CCRC, LLC, Plaintiff vs. DeKalb County Tax Assessors, Defendant. The case was decided 11/24/2008. Again, some of the details have been changed to protect my client's confidences.

months, before the first brick had been laid, the memberships were fully subscribed, and the developer collected over $50,000,000.

Memberships to the CCRC are like memberships to a golf club. They constitute an intangible asset. The courts have ruled that they do not generate a usufruct (a right to occupy another's real estate). During the case we presented evidence that the County did not pay any attention to the money generated by memberships to the privately owned golf clubs located in the County. For example, the 2,500 membership fees paid to the Capital City Club totaled $200,000,000, whereas the ad valorem property value of the golf course, according to the County Assessors, was $12,654,700.

The usual first step in the analysis of the value of the real estate, separate from the value of the intangible for an assisted living facility or a CCRC, is to value the entirety as a going concern. This approach is usually called a top-down approach.

Fortunately, there are enough sales of these types of senior living developments on a national basis to make it possible to extract a direct capitalization rate from the marketplace and to apply both an income approach and a sales-comparison approach. If the appraiser is generally unfamiliar with this property type, he or she may have to contact colleagues who specialize in this property type to get enough data to be comfortable with a going concern analysis, but that is what is required by the Competence Provision of our Standards in the first place.

In the case above I presented two methods of separating the intangible value from the value of the real estate. One was the "across the fence" method of determining the value of the most reasonable comparable real estate type property that is not also a quasi-business, quasi-real estate property. I used the "best" rental multifamily units in the County as a comparable.

The appraiser should select the most reasonable unit of comparison for this type of analysis. Sometimes $/bedroom or $/sf is a better unit of comparison than $/unit. CCRCs and other assisted living facilities often have more common area and wider hallways than typical multifamily units. However, both the income approach and the sales-comparison approach can be applied to approximate the contributory value of the real estate using the most comparable "across the fence" analogue and the appraiser can adjust for the required "extraordinary" square footage.

The second method was to either learn the business appraiser's skills or hire a business appraiser as a colleague to directly value the intangible asset and then subtract the business value from the value of the entirety as a going concern. The most problematic issue in this technique is to estimate the required return of and return on the real estate without knowing the value of the real estate in the first place. Since occupancy expense is always an operating expense to a business, an imputed rent as an expense is an essential component of the analysis of the business value.

If the facility is newly constructed, the appraiser may be able to approximate rent by determining the replacement cost of the real property and then applying a cap rate that one can extract from the marketplace for the next best analogue property type. Of course, one may have to face the problem that the real estate may not be worth what it cost to build, as shown in the CCRC example above. No one said that this stuff is easy. If it were, no one would pay us the thousands of dollars it costs to appraise these unusual assets.

If the facility has some age on it, the appraiser may wish to value the land as if vacant using the sales-comparison approach and then extract accrued depreciation from comparable sales of the next best analogue property. This technique would reduce the appraisal error to the share of the cost approach associated with the improvements.

In any case, rent must be sufficient to recover the return on and the return of the capital associated with the real estate over the remaining effective life of the asset, same as usual. The appraiser may have to estimate a range of likely rent for the subject real estate and undertake a

Monte Carlo simulation[20] to best estimate total enterprise operating expenses. It is useful to remember that capitalization rates for a business valuation are substantially higher than for real estate valuations. Consequently, the magnitude of an error in estimating occupancy expense as operating expense to the business is mitigated to some extent by the high cap rates for the intangibles.

The Importance of Multiple Techniques

I hope that anyone reading this can see the importance of using multiple techniques and multiple approaches to estimate the share of the value of a going concern that should be associated with any class of assets. At the end of the analysis the entirety of the appraisal must make sense. No rational entrepreneur would operate a CCRC that requires large numbers of trained (and often licensed or certified) employees and requires major outlays for consumables and supplies unless there was profit to be made on these activities. That profit must be over and above what the entrepreneur could earn just by owning a traditional multifamily, rental facility that did not accept a major responsibility for the care and feeding of the tenants. Consequently, there must be some earnings for the business or the analysis doesn't make any sense.

Throughout this discussion I have made light of the contribution to the overall value associated with the tangible personal property. I do not mean to imply that personal property is not an essential element. However, the tangible personal property seldom contributes a major portion of the overall value, so an error associated with the personal property probably doesn't seriously impact the overall value conclusions about the business or the real estate.

---

[20] Monte Carlo simulations are used to model the probability of different outcomes in a process that cannot easily be predicted due to the intervention of random variables. It is a technique used to understand the impact of risk and uncertainty in prediction and forecasting models.

Read more: Monte Carlo Simulation | Investopedia https://www.investopedia.com/terms/m/montecarlosimulation.asp#ixzz5KnGyCPCO ; Investopedia on Facebook

Secondly, the tangible personal property is relatively short lived. It is listed in detail of the depreciation schedule associated with the asset's IRS return. Usually there is little controversy about the remaining value of the tangible personal property as shown on the depreciation schedule, and most of the parties will agree to apply that estimate as appropriate for the appraisal. If there is controversy the issue can be settled by retaining a competent personal property appraiser.

It Is All a Matter of Degree

I think that every income-producing, real estate asset includes some business value, but, by convention, we who make up the market for real estate assets (buyers, sellers, brokers, lenders and appraisers) account for "the enterprise value of the real estate" by making an allowance for entrepreneurial profit in the cost approach, selecting comparables and /or adjusting for differences between the comparables and the subject by rental rates and by levels of occupancy and expense in the sales comparison approach, and by imputing a management fee and a reserve replacement as well as selecting operating expense comparables in the income approach.

Also, personnel management, administrative and labor costs, advertising and consumables usually constitute a relatively small percentage of total revenue for most generic forms of income-producing, real estate assets. This means that the "business" component of most of these types of real estate assets is a relatively small share of the total value of the assets. The return of capital associated with these business components has been accounted for by directly expensing them as "operating expenses," and the return on the capital associated with these intangibles is likely to be a very small portion of the capitalization rate to be applied to the residual NOI (collections net of the operating expenses).

It is only when the real estate becomes less of a generic box within which one does business and more of a specialized box through which one does business that the share of the total value of the asset as a going concern becomes large enough to become a problem for the lender, the tax assessor and the appraiser, each of whom must classify the component assets either as tangible real property, tangible personal property or intangibles.

One of the best clues that the asset type includes intangibles sufficient to require their direct consideration is in the number of people required to operate the asset (as compared to the next best, but generally agreed to be real estate only, comparative alternative – such as the comparison of the CCRC to a typical multifamily real estate asset of comparable quality). A 300-unit, multifamily complex may have a total staff of eight to ten employees in management, maintenance and administration, whereas the 300-unit CCRC required a staff of over 100. A further test is the number of employees who are state licensed or otherwise regulated or certified to perform their jobs.

Most business profits in service businesses are made from intangibles, such as an organized and trained workforce. Just consider how different the job of sales is at an apartment complex as compared to a hotel. The sales staff at the apartment complex may have to account for an average annual turnover of 80% to 120% to keep a stabilized occupancy of 90% whereas the sales staff at the hotel must sell each room every day or two or an average annual turnover of about 3000% to keep an average occupancy rate of 65% or 70%. The hotel must invest a great deal of total capital in advertising and the reservations network to keep those rooms occupied. If it is to remain a going concern, it must earn a return on that capital investment, not just the return of the direct costs of the ads and the staff as a part of the hotel operating expenses.

Another excellent clue to the status of the asset is in the cost of consumables as a percentage of total revenue. The consumables at a multifamily rental complex generally consist of a few thousand dollars for supplies for the maintenance crews and coffee and toilet paper in the clubhouse, seldom more than a few cents per square foot of the complex in the operating expense pro forma. The consumables at the CCRC include two or three meals per day for most of the residents and staff as well as bed linens and toilet paper, etc., for almost every resident. These consumables are part of the service the CCRC is in business to provide its residents and may account for 60% of total revenue. Once again, there must be a return on the capital required to provide these consumables as well as the return of that capital if the CCRC is to remain a going concern.

Senior living facilities are just one of a number of classes of quasi-real estate, quasi-business assets that real estate appraisers are often asked to appraise. Others usually include hotels, fast food restaurants, convenience stores, branch banks, funeral homes, day care facilities, miniature golf courses and other real estate improvements for which there is only a very limited adaptive reuse in the event they do not remain as a part of a going concern.

Most users of appraisal services turn to real estate appraisers when they must have a value placed on these types of assets. We have access to several market-based metrics that assist us in valuing the going concern for these types of assets. We real estate appraisers only get in trouble when we are asked to separate the going concern into the component asset classes (tangible real estate, tangible personal property, and intangibles). It is for this final step of the process that we need to make a colleague of a business appraiser and perhaps the personal property appraiser to complete the assignment.

Chapter 16: Consequential Benefits and Consequential Damages

Eminent domain gives an appraiser an opportunity to solve many interesting real estate problems because the motivations of the parties are so very different. The taking authority wants the strip of land, for example, because it wants to improve a road, and so it takes a few feet of land here or access there to comply with the road design engineer's plans. The engineer is concerned with the constraints imposed by his art and science and by the regulations of the state and Federal highway authorities.

Under the terms of the Fifth Amendment of the U.S. Constitution, and of the Constitution of the state, the public entity cannot take private property without "just and adequate" compensation having been paid. The taking agency hires a real estate appraiser to determine the market value of the property to be taken. Once it pays the money into the court, it takes title to the property. From this point on it is only a battle about how much money is required to come up with the "just and adequate" part of the compensation. The (former) property owner doesn't have the right to refuse to sell the property to the government.

The private party who owned the land didn't voluntarily list his property on the open market. He or she may have been perfectly satisfied with the road as it was. Once he was faced with the prospect that the government will take a portion of his land, he is usually more interested in the specific and unique impact that the road project will have on the remainder of his property than in the value of the part that was to be taken. This is what is meant by consequential benefits or consequential damages.

Consequential Benefits

As strange as it may seem at first blush, it is possible for an eminent domain project to specifically benefit the remaining property. Specific benefit means a benefit that is unique to that former parent parcel, not of general benefit to the population at large. Many folks will benefit from the road improvement hypothesized in my example or the highway department wouldn't undertake the improvement project in the first place. In fact, all the properties along the road may realize some increase in value because the road improved access to these properties. These are general benefits, and do not need to be taken into account.

A classical example of specific benefits that we teach in our appraisal courses is the example of a farmer with 100 acres on the edge of a growing community. Before the road project his 100 acres was worth $5,000/acre, or $500,000. The highway department decided to construct an expressway to the community and took 40 acres to build the expressway and a cross street with an expressway interchange through the farmer's property, leaving him with a remainder property made of four 15-acre parcels, each with expressway exposure and access to the new cross street. The market value of each of these 15-acre parcels suitable for hotels, restaurants and convenience stores is $1,000,000, or a total remainder value of $4,000,000 after the take.

The appraiser tasked with determining compensation for the 40 acres taken would have one of two very different rules to follow, depending on the jurisdiction of the taking authority. If this were a Federal taking, or if it were in a state that followed the Federal rule, the proper determination of compensation would follow the "before and after" rule. It this case the appraiser would say that the larger parcel (the eminent domain name for the parent parcel before the take) of 100 acres was worth $500,000 and the remainder (the eminent domain name for what was left of the parent tract after the taking) was worth $4,000,000. Since the remainder was worth more than the part taken, compensation would be $0. At least the taking agency didn't make the property owner pay the $3,500,000 increase in the value of his property, even though the property tax assessor will probably come along with a much higher property tax bill.

If the property happened to be in Georgia or one of the 20 or so other states that apply the state rule (and if it were not a Federal taking), the farmer would have to be paid for what was taken, regardless of the increase in value to the remainder. If the project was to be undertaken by the Georgia D.O.T. (GDOT), compensation would have been $200,000 ($5,000/acre for 40 acres) cash, and the fact that the remainder was worth $4,000,000 would not be considered by anyone but the property tax assessors.

Consequential Damages

Under either the Federal rule or the state rule, specific damages to the remainder property must be considered to arrive at just and adequate compensation. Once again, the damages must be specific to the parent property, not a general inconvenience to the public. Many courts have held that a fast food restaurant that used to benefit from two-way traffic cannot be compensated when the highway department constructs a median that limits the restaurant to only one-way access. Everyone is equally inconvenienced by the median (which is generally considered to be a tool for public safety, like a traffic light), not just the fast food restaurant that suffered the loss of access to about half of the traffic flowing by the restaurant.

A good example of specific consequential damages would be the case of a property owner who had a tract that had 300' of frontage and 400' of depth along a busy road. Before the take this 2.75-acre tract was a very useful commercial tract which, in many markets, could easily expect to sell for between $5/sf to $20/sf and be used for a convenience store and/or a fast food restaurant.

Suppose the highway department determined that they needed 350' of depth along that 300' of frontage, leaving a 15,000-sf tract that had 300' of frontage but a depth of only 50'. Say that the parent tract before the take was appraised at $10/sf. The taking agency would have to pay $1,050,000 for the 105,000-sf part that they took. However, the remainder would be a relatively useless tract, for it is very hard to find a commercial use for highway frontage with depth of only 50'. The only way that the owner of the parent tract can be fairly compensated is if he is also paid the difference between the value of the remainder before the take ($10/sf in this example) and the value of the remainder tract recognizing the impact of the part taken on the remainder.

Tracts that are 300' long and 50' wide very seldom sell under conditions that comply with the definition of market value. That means there is no directly comparable market data on which an appraiser can base his opinion of market value. As a consequence, the appraiser has to base his judgment on analogues and reasoning and the opinion of knowledgeable market participants. The fewer the facts, the more appraisers' opinions are likely to vary. The more the appraisers' opinions vary, the more likely it is that differences of opinion will become great enough to bring the matter to court. The following are a few examples of cases wherein the big difference of opinion rested on the different appraisers' opinions of consequential damages. All of them are associated with the same D.O.T. project and are all at the same intersection.

The 14th-Street Bridge

14th Street in Atlanta was one of only three east-west streets that bridged the I-75/I-85 canyon that divides the east side of the expressway into the rich part of Atlanta and the west side, which – for the 50 years prior to the construction of the 17th-Street Bridge – was the industrialized and much less-valuable west side of Atlanta. However, nothing remains the same forever, even in the development of a city. The Atlantic Steel Company, long a cork in the bottle for redevelopment of the west side, moved and beginning in about 1995 Atlantic Station became a "new" old-fashioned downtown for Atlanta with over 15,000,000 sf of retail, office and residential development and 11 acres of public parks and open space.

As a part of the redevelopment of the west side the Georgia DOT substantially improved the 14th- Street Bridge, widening the bridge by a couple of lanes and raising the level of the bridge and road about 12 feet. The road improvements were great for the driving public and really helped in the general redevelopment of the west side, but really put a crimp in the shopping center, restaurant and camera business located in the commercial node along both sides of 14th St. at that intersection. Snagging out 60' of the frontage of a commercial strip and raising the level of the road 12' generally has a negative impact on the folks who were trying to do business in that location.

I was involved in three of the eminent domain takings cases for this road and bridge project. They were the Silver Skillet restaurant, the Wolf Camera store and the Midtown Plaza Shopping Center. Each of these presented a very different appraisal problem and all were interesting to me.

Wolf Camera

Chuck Wolf and his cousin, David Ritz, were both in the camera store business. At its height Wolf Camera had 37 stores and Ritz about 350 stores. Wolf Camera tried to swallow up the 450-store Fox Photo chain but choked on the effort and went into bankruptcy in 2001. It was bought by Ritz, which followed it into bankruptcy in 2009, having failed to survive the switch from silver film to digital.

Up through about 2002 most of us who needed to photograph stuff used 35 mm silver-based film. Almost every appraisal we produced at PBW, Inc., required about five photographs of the subject and its neighborhood and at least one photograph of every comparable property we used, and we produced at least three copies of every report. Our production staff would spend hours in trips to Wolf Camera, sorting and labeling prints and pasting them into the reports. In 2002 our bills at Wolf Camera exceeded $20,000 for the year and we were only a modest-sized appraisal firm.

Digital cameras became less expensive and as soon as we could print reasonable images on a color printer, our lives got much better. Ritz tried to transition to a new business model by providing services such as printing custom images on tee shirts and coffee cups, but neither those services nor new equipment sales were sufficient to keep the chain out of reorganization.

My involvement with Wolf/Ritz as a client began sometime in 2005 when the Wolf store at 14th St. and I-75/85 was condemned for the 14th Street Bridge project. At that time Chuck Wolf owned the real estate (the building and about a half acre of land) and Ritz owned the business. I never could find enough value in the real estate to satisfy Chuck Wolf, so I was fired, and Chuck was his own expert at trial. Under our eminent domain procedures in Georgia, a property owner has a right to be heard by the court and does not have to qualify as an expert witness to have his opinion of just and adequate value considered. Chuck did a wonderful job for himself and was awarded several times the value my testimony could have supported.

In Georgia, Florida and in several other states, an entity whose property is condemned can make a claim for a loss in the intangible value or business value as well as the value of the real estate. This right is not universal in the country. A Federal taking expressly excludes any right to compensation for a business loss, and many states follow the Federal rule in eminent domain. However, the Georgia Supreme Court has ruled that "property" in the Takings Clause of the Georgia Constitution applies to property of all types, including the right to do business.

Consider the impact of this difference on the fate of a convenience store owner who is doing business at an expressway intersection. Suppose a new highway bridge condemned the property and there was no similar location to which the C-store could move. The landlord could be made whole by an award equal to the value of the real estate, but what about the business operator who leased the store so that he could earn 1% to 2% of the price of a gallon of the gas and 30% of the inside sales of cokes, condoms and lottery tickets? Following the take the store operator would be out of business as a direct result of the condemnation.

In Georgia the store operator could make a separate case for compensation under certain circumstances. The burden of proof switches in these cases. Under eminent domain rules the condemning authority must prove to the court that the amount of money offered for the property is equal to market value for the part taken plus damages to the remainder. To make a business loss claim the operator must prove that (1) his business had a "unique" relationship to the real estate, and (2) that as a direct result of the taking the business has suffered a permanent loss.

"Unique" itself has a specific meaning in Georgia. It does not mean that the business owner has to prove that this is the only convenience store in the state, even though the DOT's attorneys usually try to convince a judge or jury that there are lots of C-stores and there was nothing special about the one that was taken. The best discussion of "Uniqueness" I have read can be found in a monograph prepared by Charles Pursley, Esq., currently of the firm Pursley, Friezes & Torgrimson.[21] Charles is among the best respected eminent domain attorneys in Georgia, and the law book that specializes in the subject is called "Pursley on Eminent Domain." The three tests for "uniqueness" are (1) the relocation test; (2) the value to the owner test, and (3) the inadequacy of market value for just and adequate compensation. The question of eligibility for business loss is a question to be decided by the jury and there only has to be slight evidence that the issue has passed any one of these tests for the jury to consider business loss.

The Relocation Test

The case I described above is a good example of the relocation test. In the before situation the C-store had a prime-corner location at the intersection to an expressway. In the after situation someone else owns

---

[21] http://pftlegal.com/wp-content/uploads/2012/12/949289-Condemnees-Perspective-on-Met.pdf.

all the possible sites wherein the C-store could relocate. This issue first came to the attention of the Court when a liquor store at the intersection of a wet county and a dry county was condemned and could not be relocated. We no longer have many dry counties in Georgia, but it was a common situation when I first came here in 1963. Happy Herman's was at the Fulton and DeKalb County line. Fulton was wet, and DeKalb was dry. Emory U. was in DeKalb, and Happy's was the closest place we Emory students could strike a blow for liberty. DeKalb is now a wet county and Happy's is now out of business, but it was a hell of a business while it lasted.

The Value to the Owner Test

Lots of owners believe that their property has a unique value to them because it was Grandma's place or the family homestead, but these types of arguments seldom hold up in court. I think the clearest example was the case of the fellow who had a factory on one side of a busy road in a built-up section of town and the employee parking lot was on the other side of the road. Once the government condemned half of his parking lot to widen the road there was no longer any parking for his employees and he had to close the factory. Although the government paid market value for the land it took, that payment would not make the factory owner whole.

The Inadequacy of Market Value Test

One of the best examples of this test with which I was involved was the case of a fellow whose business consisted of selling decorative stone. He had an ordinary 15,000 square foot, plain vanilla, pre-engineered metal building, but he had built in about 15 fireplaces of different types of stone, six or seven different marble and granite counters and had fronted the façade of his building with about a dozen different stone treatments all to illustrate ways folks could use his products. From the point of view of market value, the appraiser would ordinarily ignore all the fireplaces, countertops and façades as "superadequacies" and determine the market value of the real estate by comparison with other 15,000 sf pre-engineered metal buildings that recently sold. However, "market value" would not treat this fellow fairly, because all the super adequate improvements were associated with his business, not with the real estate, even though they constituted part of the real estate.

There Is More To Say about Ritz Camera

Ritz's business at this Wolf Camera store location was a substantial business. This had been the top-producing store in the Wolf Camera chain and was the third, top-gross store for all the Ritz chain following Ritz's acquisition. Although revenue had been falling as digital photography made greater and greater inroads on the silver-film business, I thought the losses were stabilizing as the specialty printing side of the business increased. As it turned out, I had not realized the full impact of internet shopping and digital photography and I probably overvalued the business, but I was convinced of the rightness of my own opinion and that is what it takes to be persuasive as an expert witness.

The best break that Ritz and I had in this case was that the business appraiser that the DOT hired was overly pessimistic. The GDOT hates paying for business loss in eminent domain and will not even hire a business appraiser in a case until the business owner's attorney raises the issue in a case. Consequently, zero value ($0) was the kind of news the DOT wanted, and the DOT's business value expert testified to $0. This was in spite of the fact that the business was still generating millions of dollars in sales and throwing off hundreds of thousands of dollars of free cash flow (money left after all expenses required to keep the business going).

Zero value was the best answer that we could have gotten from the other side. Zero sounded unreasonable and unfair to the jury. Once the jury believes that a property owner is being treated arbitrarily and unfairly they tend to sympathize with the property owner.

The condemning agency's attorney's job is to persuade the jury that the condemnee is just being greedy and unreasonable, and that his appraiser is a hired gun who is trying to gouge the public. The appraiser's job is to persuade the jury that he is well prepared, careful, unbiased and reasonable. Whoever wins that battle wins the case. In this case Ritz won a substantial award, probably more than it was entitled to, as the GDOT's attorney reminds me every time we meet. After all, Ritz did go bankrupt shortly after the case, just as the GDOT's business appraiser said that it would. Remember, an expert witness's job is to be believed, not to be correct.

The Silver Skillet Grill

The Silver Skillet Grill is one of Atlanta's great olde-timey breakfast restaurants revered by politicians, businessmen and the general hoi polloi. It has been in business in the same location on south side of 14th Street for the past 60+ years. I think that it still has the same décor as it had when it opened. Most of the booths have more duct tape covering than Naugahyde. It is the type of place where if there were to be a little grease fire the flames would leap from table to table, but it serves a wonderful breakfast and lunch and is almost always filled to the brim.

The Silver Skillet is at the front end of a long, functionally obsolete warehouse, manufacturing and office building typical of the old west side Atlanta infrastructure. Most of the parking for the restaurant was along the 14th-Street frontage (to the north of the restaurant) and about 100' of the east and west side of the building. The road-widening project took about 25' of the frontage, wiping out almost all of the parking. After the take the front door of the restaurant was within 5' of the sidewalk and they had lost about 60 parking spaces. Alternative parking was possible further to the south along the east and west side of the building, but in the "after" condition, most of the parking would be a substantial walk from the front door.

Both sides' appraisers came up with about the same appraised value of the larger parcel before the take (appraisal speaks for the value of the Silver Skillet as a going concern before considering any impact of the proposed road-widening project). This was a rare enough occurrence, but what was even more surprising was that both sides' appraisers agreed that the property could "be cured" by moving the Silver Skillet back further into the underused building, redoing the interior of the restaurant, which needed it badly, chopping off the front 30' of the building and adding a new front wall. This "cure" would be less expensive than putting the restaurant out of business. The parties settled for an amount of money that would be equal to the costs of redoing the building and refurbishing the restaurant.

In eminent domain the case is over when the parties (or the court) determine just and adequate compensation. Once money is paid it is only money. The condemnee can undertake the project for which the money was paid or can pocket the money and do whatever the condemnee wants. In the "after" situation, the Silver Skillet kept the money and its customers are making do, parking wherever they can and hiking to the same old front door, which is now within a few feet of the street, in order to sit on the same old duct tape in the same old booths and enjoy the same old wonderful food.

Midtown Plaza Shopping Center

Midtown Plaza took up the north side of the 14th-Street frontage east from Techwood Drive (a one-way, southbound road that ran parallel to the I-75/85 Connector) to Fowler Street, a two-lane, residential-type street, to the west. Selig Enterprises was the principal owner of about 4.5 acres at this prime location. The Midtown Plaza Shopping Center was an approximately 50,000 sf, two-level shopping center that served as an interim use until Selig decided to redevelop the site.

The site sloped downward to the east about 25' from the main-level parking lot in front of Office Depot and Walgreen's Pharmacy to the lower-level (inferior) space rented to a used office furniture store. The primary entrance to the shopping center was from 14th St., whereas most of the customers for the lower level accessed the stores from Techwood Drive. There was an about 12'-high retaining wall between the parking lot and Fowler Street, with no Fowler Street access. I guess a picture inserted here would have saved the last 1,000 words, but I no longer have a good picture of this site as it was before the take.

The current improvements on the site only constituted an interim use, not the highest and best use of this site. The net operating income (NOI) from the operation of the center would only have supported about $5,000,000 worth of real estate, whereas all of the appraisers engaged in this assignment thought that the land alone had a market value of about $30,000,000 before the take.

The first interesting thing about Midtown Plaza was that Selig was content to continue to operate the center as an interim use, even though it did not represent the highest and best use of the land. After all, the tenants were paying all the holding costs such as debt service, property taxes, insurance, maintenance and management costs. Real estate is the type of asset that economists refer to as a "bulky good." Real estate developments take a long time to build, they are capital intensive, they require a long period before they begin to generate any cash flow, and they last a long time. The guy who builds a mega, mixed-use office, retail and residential complex just as the market demand for this type of live-work-play environment peaks is considered a genius. The guy who just misses the market goes broke. Being in a situation wherein someone else is paying all the costs to hold the property while you put together your plans, permits and capital is what defines the successful real estate developer, and Selig has been successful in Atlanta's turbulent real estate market since 1918.

The second interesting thing to me about this appraisal experience was that all the appraisers engaged for the assignment (two by the property owner's attorney and two by the DOT) agreed to the value of the larger parcel before the take. I can't stress enough how rare an occurrence this is. After all, appraisers are each supposed to be independent. I can attest from a 35+-year career in this business that all appraisers I have met are generally solitary monks who work silently in their own small cells and seldom speak to each other about the weather, never mind discuss the value of something. The joke is that you can tell the outgoing appraiser at a cocktail party because he is the one looking at your shoes rather than his own.

In any case, we all agreed about the value of the larger parcel before the take. Within a few dollars we all agreed about the value of the part taken by the DOT to widen the road. The trouble came about because we did not agree about the value of what remained following the take, which is how one makes a calculation about the extent to which the take damaged the remaining parcel. "Damages" is defined as the difference between the value of the remainder before the take (the value of the larger parcel less the value of the part taken) and the value of the remainder following the take. In this case the difference of opinion between the appraisers hired by the DOT and the appraisers hired by the property owner's attorney was north of $20,000,000.

How is it that theoretically unbiased, independent real estate appraisers can see such very different values? It is reasonable to ask: Are the appraisers in effect unbiased, independent analysts or are they just hired guns who will say anything that their client tells them to say? Let me try out the following in defense of my profession.

It is important to recognize that litigation is too risky and too expensive to be a rational alternative to negotiation unless the differences between the parties are so large that it seems better to roll the dice than to roll over.

Differences of opinion that do wind up in court are usually circumstances wherein there is a big difference of opinion and the two sides really believe in the reasonableness and factual basis of their appraiser's opinion of value, or when the property owner is indeed mad and stubborn. I must have enough faith in my opinion to be willing to stand up to the cross-examination of a well-trained, well-paid litigator hired by the other side to make me look incompetent. By law appraisers can't work under contingent fee arrangements. I can't benefit by the amount of the award, no matter how big it is. I am not willing to undergo the punishment of cross-examination just for my hourly rate. I really must believe in my opinion, but once I do, I will defend it anywhere.

If one grants for the moment that the appraisers in a big-dollar disagreement are honest and competent, the difference in their opinion must be explained by something other than the bias of the side that hired them. I contend that it is usually explained by the difference in the way that they see the functional utility of the property as affected by the condemnation.

The value of any real property is based on the utility that property offers to the economy. Most of us believe that a three-bedroom, two-bath house has more utility to a typical family than a two-bedroom, one-bath house, so the 3-2 usually sells for more than the 2-1, even if they are approximately the same size houses in the same or similar neighborhoods. A 20,000-sf office building generally sells for more than a 15,000-sf office building, all other characteristics being equal, because the additional 5,000 sf can generate additional income to the landlord. Appraisers generally consider utility under the concept of "highest and best use."

Once a parcel is developed, the highest and best use is usually the existing use until something changes. I tried to illustrate this point in the example of the software company whose land increased so dramatically following the construction of the 17th Street Bridge. Once the bridge was a reality, the utility of the land under the building increased to the point that the existing building became functionally obsolete. Market conditions can change radically and – in the time frame usually applied to real estate – quite quickly.

The highest and best use of land in a transitional market is the least well defined and hardest to prove. This makes land value most open to most controversy, and appraisers are likely to have very different opinions.

Midtown Crossing constituted exactly this type of land. Before the 17th Street Bridge was built land in that area traded at approximately $30/sf to $40/sf, and the improvements on the site marginally contributed to the value of the parcel as a whole. After the bridge that land value increased to between $100/sf and $125/sf and the buildings no longer had any contributory value. Highest and best use could only be realized if the buildings were razed and the site redeveloped with over a million sf of mixed-use development consisting of retail, office and multifamily housing.

After the take the street access to the remainder tract was extremely limited. Techwood Drive, which was the eastern boundary, had been reclassified as an expressway ramp. It looked like a regular street at its intersection with 16th Street, but by the time it reached the subject property frontage it was a no-access ramp to I-75/85 according to the Federal Highway Department. If you think the state department of transportation can be hard to deal with, try getting the Feds to change their mind.

The property also lost all access to 14th Street, which formed the southern property boundary. This was a GDOT decision. Their traffic engineers thought that any curb-cuts to the property that close to the new bridge would screw up traffic flow. The only permitted access would be from Fowler Street, the residential-type, two-lane street that formed the western property boundary. The difference in grade between Fowler Street and the existing parking lot for the shopping center is about 12 feet. A reasonable grade for a high volume commercial driveway is about a 5% grade, which means 20' of drive for each foot elevation grade change. The drive into the shopping center would have to be 240' long to make up the 12' grade difference, which is not practical. To provide any access into the site the DOT built a Z-shaped drive with a 12% grade from Fowler Street.

So, in the "after" situation, commercial vehicles could no longer access the existing shopping center and any access seemed pretty risky. The shopping center became a short-term storage facility. More importantly, in my opinion, the site changed from a $125/sf highly desirable, approximately four-acre site for a 1.5-million square-foot, mixed-use development into a $5/sf very marginal, limited-access property. The difference in value between a $125/sf site and a $5/sf site is $5,227,200/acre, or about $20,900,000 damage to the remainder property. The GDOT's appraisers said, "no harm, no foul" and nicked the remainder a couple million dollars. Thus, the impending lawsuit.

It isn't enough for me to have formed my opinion and be willing to testify. I must have evidence that non-appraisers who are the members of the jury can understand and believe. I know that if they like me and they think that I know what I am doing and that I am trying to do an honest job, they might pay attention to me as I try to explain myself. I know that if they don't like me, they will dismiss whatever I say, but even if they like me they aren't going to give my client another $20,000,000 just because I said that they should. I must show them how I got to my numbers.

Suppose I was reasonably correct in my valuation of the land before the take at $125/sf or about $5,500,000 per acre. Remember, the DOT only took about ½ acre for the road project. Why not pay the owner $2.5 million for the ½ acre and be done with it? To be able to pay the $20,000,000 for damages to the remainder property the jury would have to see that the highest and best use of the remainder had really changed dramatically.

This was a big case and the property owner was facing a big potential loss. Consequently, he was willing to spend the real money it cost to get competent experts to "prove" his position. The key experts in this case were a land-use planner/architect and a couple of independent, well-respected, real estate developers who normally were my client's competitors.

The land-use planner/architect had prepared a highest and best use development plan for the site based on the conditions before the taking. In this plan he proposed 1,500,000 sf of mixed-use, residential and retail development, with a little live-work office space. My initial value was $125/sf times 4.5 acres or $24,500,000, rounded. If one were to value this site on price per square foot of potential development density ($/sf(d)), the answer would have been $16.33/sf(d). I looked at several recently developed mixed-use major developments in Atlanta and found ample evidence to support between $14/sf(d) and $18/sf(d) based on the price paid for the site and the amount of development that was actually constructed on that site.

One should not be surprised that I was able to develop credible market evidence for a value of $16.33/sf(d) based on actual sales. After all, I had actual sales from which I had extracted my land-value estimate of $125/sf of land or $5,445,000/acre. People were willing to pay that land price because they generally saw the potential utility of the land in the same way. Utility really means what you can do with the land, or how many square feet of improvements you can put on each acre of land.

This improvement to land ratio is called a "floor area ratio" or FAR in real estate development argot. Zoning ordinances use FAR to distinguish categories of land-use intensity, so they can generally protect residential development from more intensive intrusions and encourage uses that support existing development and transportation infrastructure. The actual permitted FAR at this location was a FAR of 22, which meant that one could build 22 feet of improvement on each square foot of land, or one could build a 958,000-sf building on an acre of land if he could also meet the setbacks and open-space requirements.

In Atlanta our actual most intense developments average a FAR of about 12. We don't have 60-story buildings. The design FAR for the subject before the take was 7.65 (1,500,000 sf of density) / 196,020 sf of land = 7.65 FAR). This FAR ratio was clearly within the reasonable range indicated by other properties that had actually been developed as mixed-use developments in similar locations.

After the take 18-wheel trucks couldn't get access and the public had to use Fowler Street exclusively. The land-use planner determined that the biggest building that the site could accommodate given these restrictions was about a 55,000-sf building. That meant that at my "before" value of $16.33/sf(d) the "after" value of the site was $900,000, rounded. If one assumes that the owner would have been paid $2,500,000 for the ½ acre taken, plus another $1,000,000 for access rights and easements, the value of the "remainder before the take" would have been $21,000,000. The "remainder after the take" would have been worth $900,000. The difference between the two is the measure of damages, or $20,100,000.

Of course, there are nuances that affect the value on the $/sf(d) basis. Big buildings generally have a smaller $/sf(d) than smaller buildings owing to the efficiencies of scale associated with big, multistory buildings. However, I like to keep things as simple as possible, especially when I am presenting evidence in a big-money case, so I kept the "after" value at $16.33/sf(d), just the same as my "before" $/sf(d) valuation. Valuing something on density is an unfamiliar concept to the public and I didn't want to complicate the situation. I had actual sales of lots that were developed with approximately 55,000-sf buildings in my briefcase and they generally supported my $16.33/sf(d) valuation. I planned to pull those out only when I was being cross-examined.

In this case the only thing that changed was the highest and best use of the site, and the best evidence of that development potential was the opinion of the land-use planner/architect. So long as the jury believed him, I knew I was safe.

Experts in a professional field are one thing, but the jury really likes to hear from real people who do the work. Steve Selig's ace-in-the-hole was the fact that two of his nominal competitors, other competent and well-respected, real estate developers, were also willing to testify that in the "before" situation Steve owned one of the best redevelopment sites in midtown Atlanta, and "after" the take, the site was so badly damaged that neither of them would buy it at any price.

This case never went to trial. Both sides took all the depositions from all the experts and the developers, and then they sat down and tried to work something out. The DOT's attorneys knew the strength of the evidence that the owner could put on and they knew the magnitude of the loss that they could suffer. Steve knew that a concession on the part of the DOT that could salvage his site was to regain access to 14th

Street. That access, plus a pile of cash (but much less than the $20,000,000 it could have been) made a settlement possible. I don't know the actual details of the settlement, but I do know that Steve was so pleased with his team that he invited all his staff who worked on the project plus the experts, developers and attorneys to a great lunch at Bones, one of Atlanta's best steak houses, and we each got a pile of gift cards to other restaurants throughout the city. That was one of only two times in my 35-year career that I ever got a "thank you" from a property owner. Usually, they just paid my bill, which was thank you enough.

Chapter 17: Proximate Damages

Usually, if someone is going to be able to make a successful claim for damages, they must be able to prove that some specific party "caused" the damage and that the damage to their property was specific to them, and not remote. Most of the damage claims with which I have been involved are consequential damages arising from eminent domain actions, like the 14th Street Bridge discussed above. However, I have had a few cases of proximate damages, such as the case when an underground storage tank (UST) at a gas station leaked petroleum products into the soil and the plume extended to another person's property. Other cases involved a claim that a garbage transfer station to be built in a residential neighborhood would damage surrounding property values or that a cell tower built in a neighbor's back yard damaged the value of surrounding properties.

The appraisal problem to be solved in these cases is a "before and after" problem or a "but for" problem. If the evidence from the market shows that "but for" the proximate cause the property value would have been X, but in fact it is Y and Y is less than X, the difference between X and Y is a measure of the damage.

The trouble for the appraiser is that people have a great ability to ignore stuff that they can't see, and they get used to stuff that they can see, even if that stuff is rather ugly on first inspection. Take the case of the house impacted by the construction of a 100' cell tower on a neighbor's property. When I first saw the tower over a neighbor's fence, only about 60' from my client's back porch, there was no mistaking it for a big tree. It was impressive. It didn't bother the neighbor. It was several hundred feet from his house and mostly screened by a grove of trees, and he was getting paid several thousand dollars a year to rent the site to the cell tower company. However, my client believed that he would never be able to sell his house in the shadow of the tower, and that his property had been damaged.

Unfortunately, the market is a blunt instrument and my preliminary research was discouraging. I couldn't find any sales of houses wherein there was a cell tower less than 100' from the dwelling. The few sales I found wherein the house that sold had clear line-of-site exposure to a cell tower did not clearly indicate that they sold for a different price point than houses from which one could not see a cell tower all other factors being held constant. When I interviewed knowledgeable real estate agents and brokers, I got conflicting opinions about damage associated with the cell tower. Some said it was a disaster and others said it wouldn't cause a problem in selling the house.

Litigation is fearsome expensive. Just my preliminary research cost my client over a thousand dollars, and I had to tell him that I probably could not find sufficient evidence to support his claim. I was fired, and I do not know if the case ever went forward.

The case I was involved in that best illustrates the type of data that an appraiser must develop to have evidence for an opinion about proximity damages is associated with the Navy making noise. I have been fortunate enough to have been hired on this case three times, first in 2001, then again in 2005 and most recently in 2014. The case in chief has never been heard in court, and I am on hold while the parties pursue settlement in the present iteration of the case. Consequently, I have not revealed anything about any opinions I may have developed for this present case (or the related cases) in this section. All I want to do here is talk about the tools we used to try to develop persuasive evidence.

In 1995 a Base Realignment (BRAX) moved 10 additional squadrons of F-18 fighters to the Oceana Naval Air Station (NAS) in Virginia Beach, Virginia. Oceana, and a companion NAS called Fentress in Chesapeake, Virginia, about 40 miles away, are the primary east-coast training facilities wherein naval pilots learn how to land on an aircraft carrier. All day and night these very loud airplanes are flying touch and go from one NAS to the other. An F-18 is a very loud airplane, particularly when it is taking off and when it is landing. According to agreement among the parties all the flights were operational as of July 1999.

In 2001 a group of attorneys filed a petition for a class action lawsuit on the behalf of Virginia Beach and Chesapeake homeowners who believed that their properties had been damaged by the increase in noise associated with the increase in training flights. By my calculations, based on the petitioners' claims and the value of owner occupied real estate in the area, if the Navy lost, it would have been out over $360,000,000.

Airport noise is measured by a metric called Day-Night Level Decibel or DNL. It is a calculated metric based on the height of the airplane, the type of engines, the power settings, the angle and distance between the plane and the point on the ground and other factors. DNL for any longitude and latitude is calculated by an engineer using an approved formula. It does not result from somebody with a noise meter standing on the ground making recordings.

Because nighttime noise is considered more of a nuisance than daytime noise, DNL is weighted to enhance the impact of nighttime noise. DNL of 65 or more is considered an environmental hazard. All military and civilian airports have generated DNL maps that identify the noise-impacted areas around the airport by 5 isobar intervals. That is, lines are drawn for 65 to 70 DNL, 70-75 DNL and above 75 DNL. Less than 65 DNL is considered as ambient noise and not an environmental hazard.

DNL is a logarithmic scale wherein the level of noise doubles for every one-unit increase in DNL, so 70 DNL is a lot louder than 65 DNL and anything over 75 DNL is considered unfit for human habitation, according to the Environmental Protection Act. Consequently, owner-occupied homes around civilian airports are usually treated for sound if they are within the 65-75 DNL group and they are acquired and demolished if they are at 75 DNL or greater. My house, which was near the Atlanta Hartsfield-Jackson International Airport, was at the edge of the 65 DNL isobar once the third and fourth runways were constructed. My house, and my neighbors' houses, were all treated for noise pollution. We got storm windows and doors, extra attic insulation and, if a house didn't have central air conditioning, a new HVAC was installed. A little to the south of me an entire 350-unit subdivision was acquired and demolished. It became the site of the new College Park Convention Center and remote parking for the airport. It is still an eerie experience to drive over what used to be subdivision streets and see nothing but driveways and pads where there used to be houses.

There was no question that the Navy substantially increased the level of noise around Oceana and Fentress when it brought in the additional flights for training. Prior to 1999 65 DNL constituted the 99th percentile of noise for the area. After 1999 65 DNL constituted the 90th percentile, which meant that there were a lot more houses at 65 DNL or higher after the new flights were operational. In the "before" circumstance, the highest recorded DNL was at 74.06 DNL, whereas in the "after," the highest was 82.2 DNL.

We were one of three experts hired by the Justice Department to provide evidence in the case. In addition to ourselves, there was a local residential real estate appraiser who was hired to conduct traditional residential appraisals of an agreed-to, dozen test cases before and after the July 1999 effective date. Also, the DOJ hired a well-known econometrician who undertook both a literature search and a heuristic analysis (multilinear regression) wherein the noise level was one of the potential explanatory variables.

My job was to study the inventory of houses that sold both before and after the noise event. I was assisted in this task by Joe Katz, Ph.D., and Andy Sheppard, MAI. Joe is an applied statistician who, for many years, was a professor at Georgia State University. Andy is my former colleague at Pritchett, Ball and Wise, Inc.

We looked for the same house selling both before and after the noise event, no changes other than the market for all houses may have changed and the level of noise may have changed. We eliminated any sales that did not conform to the traditional definition of market value. That meant we did not include any house that was sold from foreclosure or in lieu of foreclosure (like a short sale). We excluded any sale from parents to children. We checked each sale to determine whether there had been any building permit pulled for improvements between the first sale and the resale. We looked forward and backward five years from the July 1999 effective date and generated a database of just under 3,700 sales and resales of the same house that met all our other criteria. We geocoded each address by longitude and latitude and obtained the "before" and "after" DNL for each house.

We merged the Virginia Beach and Chesapeake Multilist data for each house with the property tax records for each house and relied on the Multilist description of the competitive differentials that the marketplace recognized, such as the number of bedrooms and bathrooms, or a pool or a corner location or a brick façade, but we relied on the property tax card for a description of the square footage. Real estate agents and brokers know that they are liable for misinformation about a listing, so they usually describe houses based on what they can see. Real estate appraisers and tax assessors usually either measure a house's square footage or take the dimensions from approved plans. We used price per square foot ($/sf) for the unit of comparison both "before" and "after." To see whether there was any difference in the time it took to sell a noisy house as compared to a quiet house, we used the days-on-market (DOM) data from the multilist "sold" books.

There is a statistical test based on the distribution of the means and standard deviation of any set of data called the "t" test. This is a very reliable statistical test if there were as few as 30 data points in the sample size. We had almost 3,700 data points, which meant that we had enough data points to hold lots of possible differences in the market constant (such as the year the house first sold before July 1999 and the year that it sold after July 1999) and look only at differences in levels of noise and still have a statistically significant sample. Remember, we were looking at a "before" and "after" sale of the same house. If it had been a three-bedroom, two-bath brick house before the noise event, it was still a three-bedroom, two-bath brick house after the noise event.

We thought that there were three ways that an increase in noise might have affected the value of a house. (1) It may be that the value of a quiet house increased, but the value of a noisy house stayed the same or decreased. (2) It may be that the value of both the noisy house and the quiet house increased, but value of the quiet house increased at a faster rate than the rate of increase of the noisy house. (3) Finally, it may be that the value of both quiet houses and noisy houses increased at the same rate, but that the noisy house took a longer time to sell. As there is a time-value to money, if the noisy house took longer to sell, one could measure "damage" to the noisy house by discounting the sales price to the equivalent date for the quiet house.

We defined noise in two different ways. We looked at the actual DNL calculated for every address and looked at the change in $/sf and the days-on-market (DOM) for quiet houses vs. noisy houses for each DNL at 60 and above. We also calculated the change in DNL for each house by subtracting the "before" DNL from the "after" DNL. We called this the Delta DNL. We thought that if a house had gone from being a quiet house in the "before" to a noisy house in the "after" or from being a moderately noisy house (say 65-70 DNL) in the "before" to a very noisy house (say 75 DNL or above) in the "after," there might be an impact on $/sf or DOM that could reasonably be attributed to the increase in airplane noise.

I used two analytical tools to examine the almost 3,700 pairs of sales of the same house both "before" and "after" the alleged date of taking. I used the SAS statistical package, published by SAS, a well-known and well-respected analytical tool generally used by the scientific and business community to analyze large amounts of data, and I used Scenario, published by COGNOS, Inc., a data-mining software company. The SAS software permitted the use of correlation analysis and contour analysis to determine the effects, if any, of noise on the change in value of the houses.

Scenario also uses a partitioned Chi Square analysis to test data. Scenario is basically a multi-linear, regression-based model that uses a CHAID (chi square automatic interaction detection) algorithm to group ranges of the values of a variable that act the same (e.g. years 1993-1995 or 1995-2001) if the impact of "year" is found to be statistically significant, but some years have a different impact than other years. Scenario also uses a partitioned Chi Square analysis to test data represented by a label (such as a brick house or a wood-shingle-sided house), eliminating the need to create dummy variables required for a regression analysis.

My analyses using both SAS and Scenario generated very similar results. Scenario output uses a graphic "tree" format to display the relationships among variables and is generally more easily understood by readers who are not trained in statistics. I use the Scenario output to illustrate the relationship of the significant variables when I believe that the data can be best understood graphically rather than numerically. However, I relied on and reported the statistics generated by the SAS analysis as the primary evidence for my opinions.

A statistical hypothesis test is a test between two competing hypotheses, the null hypothesis and the alternative (research) hypothesis. A null hypothesis is the opposite of the research hypothesis. In this case, the research hypothesis is that an increase in noise "causes" a decrease in property values. Consequently, the critical null hypothesis is that an increase in noise does not cause a decrease in property values. If one can reject this null hypothesis, one can accept the alternative (research) hypothesis that a change in noise is related to (causes) a change in value.

A statistical test requires the analyst to specify what is called the significance level to reject the null hypothesis.[22] The significance level

---

[22] In a statistical test, sample results are compared to possible population conditions by way of two competing hypotheses: the null hypothesis is a neutral or "uninteresting" statement about a population, such as "no change" in the value of a parameter from a previous known value or "no difference" between two groups; the other, the alternative (or research) hypothesis is the "interesting" statement that the person performing the test would like to conclude if the data will allow it. The p-value is the probability of obtaining the observed sample results (or a more extreme

describes the researcher's tolerance that one will reject a true null hypothesis. It is set by the researcher prior to undertaking the analysis. The significance level corresponds to the "statistical standard of proof," as the lower the significance level, the tougher the standard of proof. The usual levels of significance are at 0.05 (which Scenario refers to as a "test" analysis) and at 0.01 (which Scenario refers to as a "certify" analysis). In this case I set the level of significance at 0.05, which is generally accepted as the standard for social science research.

To sum up, I calculated the degree of linear correlation, "r", between noise (as measured by DNL) both before and after the relocation of the F/A-18 C/D aircraft and the average annual change in the value of a house for sales and resales of the same house, excluding non-third-party sales, excluding houses that had undergone rehabilitation and excluding a very few cases of extreme change in value (three standard deviations or more). I also calculated the linear correlation, "r", between noise and the days-on-market (DOM) for these same paired sales wherein I had sufficient data to calculate the DOM.

I calculated the correlation statistic "r" between the noise variables and the value variables using the SAS program. Based on the calculated value of "r" SAS calculated a test statistic "t" using the formula $t = (n-2) \frac{1}{2} (r^2 / 1 - r^2) \frac{1}{2}$. This statistic comes from a t distribution with n-2 degrees of freedom, where "r" is the sample correlation. This "t" distribution is a well-known distribution.

In statistical significance testing, the p-value is the probability of obtaining a test statistic result at least as extreme as the one that was observed, assuming the null hypothesis is true. Many common statistical tests, such as chi-squared tests or Student's t-test, produce test statistics which can be interpreted using p-values.

To sum up, SAS calculates the p-value for each of the relationships

result) when the null hypothesis is true. If this p-value is very small, usually less than or equal to a threshold value previously chosen called the significance level (traditionally 5% or 1%), it suggests that the observed data is inconsistent with the assumption that the null hypothesis is true, and thus that hypothesis must be rejected, and the other hypothesis accepted as true.

that are tested. The p-value, which is between 0 and 1, measures the strength of the evidence against the null hypothesis; the smaller the p-value, the stronger the evidence against the null hypothesis. I established a significance level of 0.05 for the test, which meant that I rejected the null hypothesis (that there is no relationship between noise and value) if the calculated p-value is less than 0.05.

I hope that the description of the type of research that was required to make any determination about the possible impact of noise (which was a proximate damage) on the value of houses illustrates the analysis required to solve this type of appraisal problem. Our appraisal fee for this work was substantially more than $100,000, and we were only one of three different types of experts that the Justice Department hired. These types of expenses are only possible in cases wherein the differences between the parties are very big sums, which is seldom the case for most proximate damage situations.

Chapter 18: Business Loss

Businesses are intangible assets. Business appraisal is a related, but separate discipline from real estate appraisal. Many of the lines of reasoning used by both real estate appraisers and business appraisers are similar, but the sources of data and the training in the methodologies are different enough that most real estate appraisers shy away from any opinion of the value of an intangible asset. Most business appraisers stay away from real estate valuation because all 50 States have passed laws requiring that real estate appraisers be licensed. The trouble comes about because the real world seldom makes perfect divisions into categories.

Most of the time, if the subject of the appraisal is a residence or a typical commercial building (like an office, retail or industrial building), most of the value is associated with the land and the improvements. The real estate appraiser gets rid of intangibles with an allowance for "management" in the income approach and an estimate of "entrepreneurial profit" in the cost approach. The sales comparison approach compares the subject with the sales of "comparables," and any value associated with brand or other intangibles is taken care of by the selection of the comparables or the adjustments to the comparables that make up the appraiser's art.

Unfortunately, there are several types of appraisal assignments wherein the asset has a large component of intangible value. Consider the situation of a full-service, branded hotel, like a Hilton or Ritz Carlton. In addition to renting rooms, these facilities have major profit centers in catering, bars and restaurants, convention centers and other amenities, each of which may be more appropriately appraised by a business appraiser than a real estate appraiser. A restaurant may rent a box worth $1,000,000 as real estate, but the business of the restaurant may be worth $3,000,000 or $5,000,000. Other types of assignments with substantial overlap are nursing homes or continuous-care, retirement communities (CCRCs), hospitals, and most properties (like fast food restaurants or convenience stores) wherein the design of the real estate is so closely associated with the business that there is relatively little adaptive reuse if the business moves out.

The real estate required to support the business is always an expense to the business, without regard to whether the business rents or owns the real estate. Rents are easy. The business treats the rent as an operating expense. A property that the business owns may be more problematic. The real estate may show up on the balance sheet as an asset, and the company may expense depreciation, but depreciation and occupancy expense are seldom the same. All these issues are why appraisers actually earn their living.

Most of the time the intended use of the appraisal is to support a loan. In the vast majority of cases both the lender and the appraiser have a common understanding of the underwriting standards for the various property types and issues about intangibles are subsumed in the underwriting process. These "conventions" permit the lender and the appraiser to assume that a hotel requires a 12% "management fee" or that a C-store value is 3X inside sales plus the 2% margin on the gas pumped. None of these "understandings" help if the appraiser is to testify about the value of a C-store in condemnation proceedings. Depending on the state, the business value of the convenience store may or may not be included in the valuation. About half of the states permit the condemnee to claim business damages in addition to the real estate, and in the other half of the states and for Federal takings, the value of the intangible asset is not compensable. I don't know why the Feds and the states that follow the Federal Rule for condemnation don't consider business loss. You would have to ask the Supreme Court. They have decided this issue a couple of times.[23]

Regardless of whether one must exclude the value of the business or

---

[23] See REAL ESTATE VALUATION IN LITIGATION, J. D. Eaton, MAI, American Institute of Real Estate Appraisal, Chicago, 1982. pp. 118-119, 165-166.

include it as an element of just and adequate compensation, the appraiser has to be able to decide how much the business is worth. When one is expected to testify in court as an expert witness, one is expected to know what one is talking about. To overcome this problem, I decided to become competent in both disciplines, which led to lots of assignments in addition to eminent domain condemnations.

Appraising an Adult Enterprise

One afternoon I received a call from an attorney who represented a minority shareholder in a privately held company. His client owned a 20% interest in a Georgia-registered, privately held corporation. The 80% owners had found a buyer for the company, lock, stock and barrel, and they didn't want to pay 20% of the proceeds of the sale to this minority stockholder. In Georgia, and in most states, a minority shareholder is protected under "oppressed shareholder" rules. If a court finds that the majority has forced a minority shareholder out of the company, the minority shareholder must be paid the pro rata value of the market value of the company.

The attorney wanted me to determine the *market value* of the company as a whole, the value of the 20% pro rata share of the stock without any discount for lack of marketability or lack of control and testify to my opinions in Superior Court. The assignment was typical. The business was not.

The company in question was housed in a windowless, block building with a parking lot and main entrance to the rear of the building. It was a "full-service, adult-entertainment" enterprise. "Adults" could purchase sexually explicit videos, books and paraphernalia suitable to any taste or gender preference, and they could view videos in the relative privacy of several, closet-size booths. An enterprise of this type is known in-the-trade as a "jack shack."

Following USPAP requirements I told the attorney that I had never appraised this type of business before, but that I believed I could learn enough to prepare a credible appraisal. It is not unusual for a business appraiser to be faced with a type of business that he has never appraised before. After all, the North American Industrial Classification System (NAICS) classifies thousands of different types of businesses. Part of a business appraiser's training is to learn how to research industries to the point of understanding the value drivers and the competitive differentials.

As I undertook industry research, I learned that the adult entertainment business is no less well organized than the convenience store business or the fast food franchise business. They have published catalogues and multiple product websites and wholesalers. They have a major industry trade show annually in Las Vegas.

My town, Atlanta, has a sufficient supply of adult entertainment businesses to prevent any monopoly pricing and to provide the appraiser the opportunity to "shop the competition" to determine the subject business's general place in the industry. A business appraiser has to make a judgment about where the business he is appraising fits into the continuum of quality and to identify the competitive differentials that may affect value. I had to inspect enough of these shops to determine whether my subject was an inferior, about average, or superior adult entertainment enterprise.

Just about the time that I was hired for this assignment I was inaugurated as President of the Atlanta Chapter of The Appraisal Institute. The Atlanta Chapter is one of the largest chapters in the country, and we were fortunate to have the National President of the Institute to swear the new officers in at our inauguration meeting.

This is a big deal for us appraisers. As a part of the ceremony the National President reminded me, as incoming Chapter President, that I was the face of the Appraisal Institute for Atlanta and most of Georgia, and that the probity of my personal and professional behavior represented and affected the public reputation and public trust for all appraisers.

In my acceptance speech I explained that in addition to being a real estate appraiser, I was also a business appraiser and that my practice was primarily oriented to disputes that wound up in court. I told them that I had been retained to value an oppressed shareholder's interest in an adult entertainment enterprise, so that if anyone saw me or my car at one of these establishments, I was only conducting due diligence research!

Most of the adult entertainment stores were relatively small establishments, generally between 1,500 sf to 3,000-sf buildings, even if they were part of a national chain. Apparently, the "big box" business model that has rolled up most neighborhood office supply stores or pet shops or hardware stores is not a suitable business model for the adult entertainment business.

My "careful" examination of the subject and the competition revealed that there was only one unusual characteristic about the store I was appraising as compared to most similar stores in Atlanta. My store had dedicated about 20% of its floor space to a line of business called "live modeling," but that profit center generated less than 1% of its revenue.

In most "live modeling" establishments a sheet of Plexiglas subdivides a closet-size space into an area occupied by the patron and the component occupied by the model. The customer feeds a money machine, a curtain raises and the model "models." In our store the owners had done away with the Plexiglas separation, which, I am sure, was a convenience to both the patron and the "model" and saved a capital expense, somewhat offset by the purchase of couches.

The unusual characteristic, from my point of view as a business appraiser, was that according to the company's books, the "modeling" profit center generated only about $18 sales for each sf of floor space, whereas the video booths and the videos and paraphernalia generated between $350/sf and $400/sf in sales. Sales of $350/sf were typical for the industry.

One of the standard assumptions an appraiser makes when he estimates *market value* is that the enterprise has typically competent management. I didn't think that any typically competent adult enterprise manager would dedicate 20% of his sales space to a business line that generated only about 0.5% of the sales that he experienced throughout the balance of the store. Some nominal space may be dedicated to a loss leader to attract customers, but never 20%. Small company books are very seldom audited, so they can't be considered as reliable as audited financial statements, and it was possible that there was some barter going on that wouldn't be recorded on the company books.

In my appraisal of the market value of the enterprise I assumed that an economically motivated, rational, competent management would replace "modeling" with a more profitable line and generate $350/sf for that space. Consequently, I increased pro forma revenues by about 20%.

Market value always reflects the anticipated future benefits of ownership. The operating history of a business or a real property provides clues to the stabilized earnings most likely to be realized from ownership, but the "willing buyer" is always looking to the future. That is why real estate appraisers and business appraisers develop pro forma estimates of stabilized future earnings.

In court we learned that the only difference between my appraisal and the appraisal prepared by the appraiser hired by the opposing counsel was associated with this 20% increase in earnings. I had explained my reason for the pro forma increase in earnings to the jury in direct testimony. In fact, the new owner of the store had replaced the "modeling" booths with additional video booths and was generating about $350/sf in sales from the converted space.

I survived most of my cross-examination intact, but, just as he was finishing, opposing counsel stopped directly in front of the jury and pointed to me and said: "I have just one more question. Mr. Wise, isn't it true that you took this company's earnings and sales as actually reported on their books and just jacked them up?" I had to drop my notes and hide below the witness box. It isn't appropriate for a witness to guffaw in front of a jury.

Chapter 19: Bond Financing Leaseholds

One of the more unusual (and, fortunately, one of the longest lasting) assignments I have ever had grew out of a dispute between a county's Development Authority and the county's taxpayer association. Like most larger local governments throughout the country, this county had a state-authorized tax-exempt local Development Authority. The authority's mission was to increase the tax digest and to increase locally based employment. To accomplish these goals, the state granted the authority tax-exempt status and gave it the right to issue bonds. In many cases the bonds are taxable bonds backed up by the projects that they fund, not by the full faith and credit of either the municipality or county or the state.

The way that the bonds work is that a developer petitions the Development Authority to issue bonds to fund a project, say a new apartment complex or mixed-use development, to replace a worn-out building or a vacant lot currently being used as a surface parking lot. The developer commits to increasing the tax digest by the value of the new project and by providing a certain number of construction and permanent jobs associated with the project. If the Development Authority agrees, it issues bonds sufficient to finance the project and accepts the title to the project for the life of the bonds. It agrees that the rent for the project will be equal to the amount to retire the bonds, plus a small management fee to the Development Authority. The developer signs a lease with terms and conditions equivalent to the terms and conditions of the bonds.

The bonds, once issued, are merchantable liquid intangible assets, generally similar to tax-exempt municipal bonds, but the sale of these bonds is restricted to knowledgeable investors with certain specified minimum net worth and the interest earned on the bonds is taxable. In almost all cases the developer buys the bonds and pledges them as security against third-party financing. Consequently, the developer gives up title to the property for the life of the bonds, but as the bondholder receives the proceeds of the "rent" paid to the Development Authority to retire the bonds and as the tenant pays that same "rent" essentially to itself, with the Development Authority acting as an intermediary, no cash rent need ever change hands. To keep everything on the up-and-up, the Development Authority hires a third-party trustee, usually a major bank, to process all the (paper) payments.

It is reasonable to ask why in the world would a developer jump through all these relatively expensive hoops to obtain bond financing? I think that there are at least three reasons:

(1) Because the bonds are liquid assets, lenders prefer them to real estate as security for a loan. They can often loan against the bonds at a higher loan-to-value ratio, and they may not have to retain as much capital against their balance sheets. The Development Authority is willing to subordinate its position as title holder to the lender, so the lender also takes a lien against the real estate as well as against the bonds.

(2) Because the bonds are classed as liquid assets rather than real estate, the developer may be able to go to only one lender for one-stop shopping for his financing. There may not be any need for construction loans to be taken out by permanent loans and no need for mezzanine financing, which is expensive in terms of both time and money.

(3) [And this is probably the most important reason] The title is held by the Development Authority, which is exempt from local property taxes. Georgia's courts have ruled that only the leasehold is subject to property taxes during the life of the bonds.[24] As the value of a leasehold is usually less than the value of the fee simple interest, property taxes for the development will be lower than otherwise so long as the Development Authority holds the title.

Before they can be issued, the bonds must be confirmed in open court in a civil bench trial prosecuted by the state's Attorney General

---

[24] *DeKalb County Board of Tax Assessors v. W.C. Harris & Co.*, 248 Ga. 277 (1981).

and defended by the Development Authority and the developer. Notice of the hearing must be properly posted and any taxpayer in that jurisdiction may intervene if they object. Once the judge approves of the bonds they are immune from any future challenge for any reason, so long as the issue has been considered by the judge during the hearing.

In the jurisdiction wherein I was hired, the Development Authority typically issues bonds with a 10-year repayment schedule and the Board of Tax Assessors (BOA) and the Authority have agreed via a Memorandum of Agreement (MOA) that the value of the leasehold in the first year of the completion of the bond-financed project is to be 50% of the fair market value of the fee simple interest in the underlying real estate asset, to be increased by 5%/year until it reaches 100% of the market value of the fee simple interest at the end of the tenth year of the lease, at which time the bonds are repaid and the title to the property reverts to the tenant (developer). This agreement as to the appropriate value of the taxable leasehold each year of the lease is generally called "the ramp-up method."

Under Georgia law all real property must be appraised at fair market value as of January 1 of each tax year, and all property is assessed at 40% of its fair market value. All property that is not tax exempt must be treated equally. In most metropolitan counties in Georgia property taxes are generally set at about 50 mills on a 40% assessment, or about 2% of the fair market value of the underlying real estate asset. Consequently, if the leasehold in a $100,000,000 bond-financed project is taxed at 1% or $1,000,000 and the neighboring $100,000,000 development is being taxed $2,000,000 based on the fee simple value, somebody might think this situation is unfair and take umbrage, or even better, might sue, which is how and why I was hired.

In 2009 John Sherman, representing himself and the Fulton County Taxpayers Association, intervened in a bond hearing claiming that the arrangement between the developer the Development Authority and the BOA was a fraud and as a result real property was not being taxed equitably as required by Georgia law. This lawsuit put in question about 20 years of bond-financed projects totaling over $50 billion. Sherman hired one of my well-respected appraisal colleagues who opined that the "ramp-up" method was a crock, and not based on any generally accepted appraisal methodology! This suit, and a subsequent follow-up suit, went to the Georgia Supreme Court twice before being finally settled in 2015.[25]

On the face of it, the idea that the value of a leasehold on a 10-year lease is 50% of the value of the fee simple interest, 55% in the second year, 60% in the third year, increasing by 5%/year does sound a little arbitrary. Consequently, it might be useful to think about the value of a leasehold as compared to the value of the underlying asset, and to see why my opinion prevailed in this set of cases.

Because properties are valued for property tax purposes in Georgia as of January 1 of each tax year, the solution to the appraisal problem requires a consideration of three issues as of January 1 for each year of the lease: (1) the value of the purchase option (if any); (2) the value of any difference between the contract rent and market rent; and (3) the value of the reversionary interest to the tenant.

Addressing the Issue of the Value of the Purchase Option

In each of these lease agreements the tenant has the right to purchase the title for $10, provided all the bonded indebtedness has been repaid. In my opinion the option to purchase the subject property for a nominal sum has no monetary value and does not contribute to the value of the taxable leasehold for the leases in question.

If the lease is still in effect as of January 1, a taxable leasehold exists as of that date. The most probable estimate of future cash flows from the lease are the terms and conditions within the lease as of January 1. If the lease is still in place and the reasoning that supports the ramp-up formula is sound, the Board of Assessors should apply the ramp-up

---

[25] *SJN Properties, LLC v. Fulton County Board of Assessors et al.* No. S14A1493, Decided: March 27, 2015. The original suit was *Sherman v. Fulton County Board of Assessors et al.* No. S10A0924, Decided: November 1, 2010. Mr. Sherman became ill in the intervening years and was replaced.

184 | It's Only an Opinion

formula described in the MOA for that year of the lease to the fee simple value of the property to approximate the market value of the taxable leasehold. If, during the year, the tenant repays the bonds and exercises the option, fee simple interest in the property will transfer to the tenant. As of January 1 the next tax year, the tax assessment will be based on a 40% assessment against 100% the fee simple value of the property, the same as it is for any other property. The taxable leasehold will have been extinguished with the repayment of the bonds and the termination of the lease.

Most of these leases contain a purchase option for $10 provided all the bonds have been repaid. But, because the purchase option can be exercised only if the bonds have been repaid, I believe that there can be no financial value to the purchase option. It is true that by repaying the bonds and exercising the purchase option earlier than the 10-year life of the bonds the developer can regain title to the real estate. However, he has gained no financial advantage and the exercise of the option removes the lease, which removes the leasehold, which removes the property tax advantage.

Contract Rent and Market Rent

The value of the leasehold associated with any below-market contract rent as compared to annual market rent for a similar real estate asset is a much more speculative problem to solve. After considering the potential variables as listed below, however, I believe that there is unlikely to be any marketable value associated with a potential difference between contract rent under the lease and market rent.

The contract "rent" is set at an amount equal to debt service based on 100% financing, including a small administrative payment to The Authority. The amortization period and the term of the lease is 10 years. At the termination of the lease, by which point all bonds must be retired, the title in the property reverts to the tenant, not the landlord.

As such the subject's contract rent cannot reasonably be compared to a market made up of leases of similar properties wherein the tenant vacates (or renews) at the termination of the lease and the property reverts to the leased fee owner.

The lease in these cases is most similar to a sale-leaseback transaction wherein the fee owner "sells" the property to an investor and leases the property back over a multiyear period. At the end of the lease the fee simple title is transferred back to the "tenant" for a nominal fee.

The contract "rent" in a sale-leaseback is generally equal to the debt service required to amortize the capital over the life of the lease, and the interest rate is usually based on the bond rating of the tenant. As such, the typical sale-leaseback conditions are mirrored by the Development Authority's lease conditions. The exception is that the term of a typical sale-leaseback lease is 20 or 30 years, whereas the Development Authority's lease runs for 10 years during which period 100% of the bonds must be repaid.

Every year the County tax assessors must value the fee simple interest in the subject, just as they do for all property on the County's digest. As a part of that process they undertake an income approach to value wherein they must make some judgment about market rent. Market rent in this context will probably be best indicated by the amount a third-party tenant would pay for similar space in, say, a new apartment building in Midtown Atlanta. This rent will be limited by the competitive alternative rents at other similar real estate in the same submarket. Contract rent, however, is the rent that the company must pay to retire 100% of the bonds in 10 years.

Real estate improvements have expected lives of 30-plus years and are generally financed for between 20 and 30 years. It would not be possible to find a leasehold advantage in rent required to repay capital in 10 years at a lower rate than the amount to repay capital over 20 or 30 years.

If, in the process of the annual appraisal for tax purposes, the assessors discovered there was a substantial increase in "market rent" as compared to the actual contract rent at the subject, the impact of that higher rent would be reflected in a higher appraisal of the market value of the subject's fee simple interest. The base against which the County's formula for valuing the leasehold would be increased. Consequently, the amount paid in property tax for the taxable leasehold would be increased.

I have constructed the following pro forma analysis to illustrate this problem. This pro forma is reasonably based on current market conditions for new multifamily development in Atlanta. It is an illustration of the impact of rent on cash flow. It is not an appraisal of the facility. I set the "value" at the $100,000,000 proposed bonded indebtedness. The analysis begins with a simple direct capitalization of the value of the fee simple interest, which is the type of analysis the tax assessors would undertake annually:

BOND FINANCE LEASEHOLD EXAMPLE						LEASEHOLD ANALYSIS INTEREST ONLY, ZERO REPAYMENT	
			FEE SIMPLE ANALYSIS				
		AVERAGE	MONTHLY PER				
Potential Gross Income (PGI)	UNITS	UNIT SF	UNIT	ANNUAL			
Rental Units	275	1047	$2.75	$9,501,525			
Retail		4,000	$35.00	$140,000			
				$9,641,525			$9,641,525
LESS VACANCY AND COLLECTION LOSS			8%	($771,322)			($771,322)
EFFECTIVE GROSS INCOME (EGI)				$8,870,203			$8,870,203
OPERATING EXPENSES, EXCLUDING RENT		28%	($2,483,657)		28%	($2,483,657)	
RENT			0%			($4,000,000)	
LESS TOTAL OPERATING EXPENSES (OE)				($2,483,657)			($6,483,657)
NET OPERATING INCOME (NOI)				$6,386,546			$2,386,546
OVERALL CAP RATE (OAR)			6.35%			6.35%	
VALUE ESTIMATE	BONDS			$100,498,696			$37,554,693
VALUE ESTIMATE, ROUNDED	$100,000,000			$100,000,000			38%

The only difference between valuing the leasehold and valuing the fee simple interest using the income approach is that one must account for rent paid by the leasehold to the leased fee as a component of the leasehold's operating expenses to determine the net operating income (NOI) to the leasehold position. Any increase in operating expense causes an offsetting decrease in NOI. As one can see from the pro forma for the fee simple position, NOI is approximately $6,390,000; which is sufficient to support a value of $100M, which is the value of the bonds.

However, if the bonds are to be repaid in 10 years, and if the rent associated with this arrangement must retire the bonds in 10 years, annual rent would have to be $10,000,000 even if the interest rate were zero (0). This is more than the remaining NOI. Even if "rent" were interest only, and the bonds were never repaid, rent would be $4,000,000 (4% of $100M), which would reduce NOI to the leasehold position to approximately $2,390,000, indicating that the value of the leasehold was about $37.5M assuming no change in the CAP rate. $37.5M is only 38% of the value of the fee simple interest. The ramp-up formula starts with 50% of the fee simple value.

I believe that this pro forma example illustrates that whereas the tax assessors can apply an income approach to appraise the value of the fee simple interest annually during the life of the lease, it will not aid them in determining the annual value of the leasehold. The only tool that they could apply would be a discounted cash flow (DCF) analysis. That technique shows that the ramp-up method is a reasonable proxy for a calculation of the annual value of the leasehold.

Addressing the Value of the Reversion

I think that all the leasehold value in these leases is associated with the reversionary interest at the end of the lease term. As each year passes and the tenant's right to acquire fee simple ownership (the title) of the property nears, the present value of the reversion increases. Hence, in each year of the lease, the value of the leasehold interest to the tenant increases.

Real estate improvements and equipment are wasting assets, and that means that the market value of those assets will depreciate year-by-year. At the same time, inflation and changes in market conditions will also cause changes in value over time. I have no way of knowing what the market value of the reversionary interest will be at the termination of the 10-year lease. However, I do know that according to the terms of the MOA, 100% of whatever is that market value (as determined by the tax assessors) will be subject to ad valorem taxes, and regardless of the market value of those assets 100% of the bonds must be repaid, even if the remaining value of the bonds exceeds the market value of the property.

Present value is calculated in terms of the present value of $1 using the formula $PV = 1/(1+i)^n$, wherein i=yield and n=the number of periods (years) remaining before the benefit of fee simple ownership can be recognized. This makes PV equivalent to a percentage. The ramp-up formula is expressed in terms of percentages. Consequently, the analytical model I developed makes it possible to compare the calculated PV percentages to the percentages in the ramp-up formula.

In this analysis I used a 4% nominal cost of capital, or whatever is the interest rate specified in the bond the Authority proposes to issue in each case. The bond repayment schedule is usually a 10%/year principal reduction plus interest on the remaining balance. The internal rate of return for this principal reduction repayment schedule is approximately equal to a 6.35% yield or discount rate (after including the benefit to the tenant of the reduction in property taxes net of the cost of the fee to the Development Authority).[26]

Below is a table showing the present value of $1.00 (equal to the taxable leasehold interest at the beginning of each lease-year over a ten-year period using a discount rate ranging from a low of 5% to a high of 10% when all the value is in the reversion). The "ramp-up" methodology to be applied by the Board to calculate fair market value of the taxed leasehold was reasonably approximated by the present value factor associated with a 7% internal rate of return for each year of the lease.

---

[26] In some cases, the bonds are interest only with a balloon at the end of the 10th year. If that is the case, the IRR is reduced by about 75 basis points to about 5.42%, all other variables held equal.

Bond Financing Leasehold Example

				Discount Rate			
	5%	6%	7%	%	8%	9%	10%
# of Years Before Reversion		PV FACTOR		Ramp Up Schedule		PV FACTOR	
10	61%	56%	51%	50%	46%	42%	39%
9	64%	59%	54%	55%	50%	46%	42%
8	68%	63%	58%	60%	54%	50%	47%
7	71%	67%	62%	65%	58%	55%	51%
6	75%	70%	67%	70%	63%	60%	56%
5	78%	75%	71%	75%	68%	65%	62%
4	82%	79%	76%	80%	74%	71%	68%
3	86%	84%	82%	85%	79%	77%	75%
2	91%	89%	87%	90%	86%	84%	83%
1	95%	94%	93%	95%	93%	92%	91%
0	100%	100%	100%	100%	100%	100%	100%

Based on average rates of returns (discount rates) reported for various property types, the above table represents what an investor might expect over a ten-year period.

A rate of return on investment (discount rate) is the percentage of dollars earned each period quoted on a present-value basis.

The 'ramp up' table used by Fulton County to value a leasehold interest fairly depicts a property's value at each year during the lease by calculating the present worth of the reversion (value at end of lease) in present-value terms based on an approximate average return (discount rate) of approximately 7%.

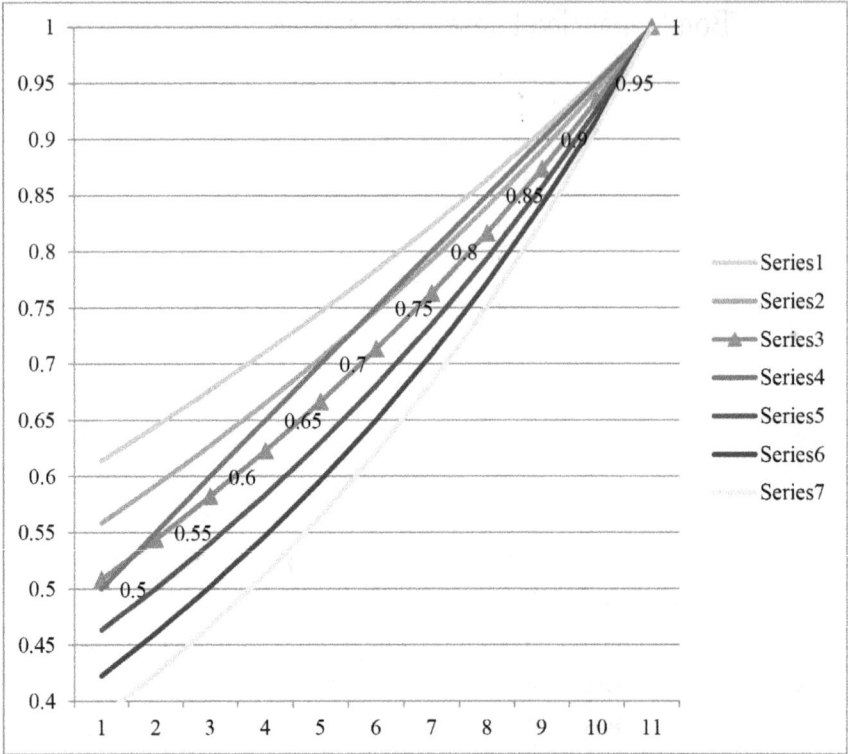

Note: Straight line = tax formula. Closeness of lines shows that the tax formula is a reasonable proxy.

The formula in the MOA reasonably reflects the appropriate present value factor expressed as a percentage for each year of the lease for any discount rate that is a reasonable estimate of the market-based, bond-financed cost of capital likely to be available that year of the lease. The "ramp-up" schedule in the MOA is very close to a discount rate of between 7% and 8%. Thus, in my professional appraisal opinion, the "ramp-up" formula that the Board employs represents an appropriate, reasonable and non-arbitrary, simplified method of arriving at the fair market value for tax purposes of the leasehold interest created by these bond-financed developments.

Chapter 20: Easements

An easement is a property right granted (or taken) by some entity that encumbers the property owned by another party. According to the free legal dictionary, an easement is the right to use the real property of another for a specific purpose. The easement is itself a real property interest, but legal title to the underlying land is retained by the original owner for all other purposes.[27] Most of the time I have been asked to opine on the value of an easement that provides either temporary or permanent access, usually on the behalf of a highway department or for a subterranean pipeline, but I have been asked about the value of an easement to permit airplanes to fly over property, which is called an avigation easement.

Valuing an easement is always a difficult assignment because it calls for a decision about the extent to which the easement affects the functional utility of the land within the easement and the extent to which (if any) it damages the remaining unencumbered property. Whenever the degree of appraisal judgment is a large component of the answer relative to the facts upon which that judgment is based, the opportunity for disagreement is greater. Easement valuations always contain a much greater portion of appraiser judgment relative to the facts.

If the DOT engineers believe that portions of your land are too close to an intersection or otherwise constitute a safety hazard, they may also condemn your rights of access on specific portions of your property. Access rights are parts of the bundle of real estate rights, and the appraisal problems associated with access rights are like the problems associated with easements, so I have included a discussion of access

---

[27] *Legal-dictionary.thefreedictionary.com/easement.*

rights in this section of the book.

Usually, if the Department of Transportation (DOT), or the "Demons of Torment" as one little old lady condemnee I worked for in Augusta, GA called them in a poem she sent to the Governor, wants some of your property to expand a road, they will condemn the fee simple interest in the right-of-way that they want for the road, but they will often condemn a permanent easement for the construction and maintenance of slopes and a temporary easement to rebuild driveways to reconnect the balance of your land to the new roadway.

Temporary Easements

To my way of thinking, temporary easements are among the easiest forms of easements to value. Temporary easements, by definition, exist only for a specified amount of time. The type of temporary easement one typically encounters is a construction easement for a specified period, say three years. The critical factor in the valuation of the temporary easement is the expected period that the easement will be in effect.

Because the property owner only gets one chance for "just and adequate compensation," and because that chance comes at the front end, when no one really knows how long the project will take or to what extent the property owner will really be inconvenienced, I think it best to use as long an estimate of the time for the temporary easement as possible. If the DOT engineers are indefinite or uncertain, the property owner should hire his own expert to provide an estimate of the likely time for construction. The expert's opinion of the expected time for construction won't be expensive relative to the award the condemnee may be seeking, and the appraiser must have reliable evidence upon which he can base his estimate of the length of time the easement will apply.

Appraisers can't be qualified as construction experts based on their appraisal training, education and experience. We can only be qualified as valuation experts. Consequently, the appraiser can't rely on his own opinion of the required time. The property owner may be able to testify as to his own opinion of the time required, but the owner's testimony won't be given much weight unless the owner can persuade the court that he knows what he is talking about.

The reason that time makes such a big difference is that the method an appraiser uses to value a temporary easement is to first appraise the land within the temporary easement before the taking and then apply an estimate of the annual rent appropriate for that land value. Suppose the DOT wanted a three-year temporary easement on a strip of land that was 435.6 feet long and 100 feet wide, or 43,560 square feet (an acre), and suppose the appraiser had sufficient evidence to appraise the subject land at $100,000/acre in fee simple, and further suppose that the appraiser believed that the market evidence supported a land-use rent of 10%/year, or $10,000/acre rent per year. Under these circumstances reasonable compensation for the three-year taking of the temporary easement would be $30,000.

If the DOT engineers estimated that construction would probably take two years, but the owner's expert thought that four years was a more reasonable estimate of the construction period, the value of the temporary easement would range somewhere between $20,000 and $40,000. This $20,000 difference of opinion isn't big enough to warrant going to court, but it is big enough to pay attention to in the negotiations. Remember, the value of the temporary easement is likely to be only a small part of a much larger difference of opinion about the just and adequate compensation for a condemnation.

Whenever I was asked by the DOT to value a temporary construction easement, I was reminded that the condemnee was to be paid up front for (let's say) three years of land-use rent, so there should be a discount. This is a classic definition of present value. Since there is a time value of money, the DOT's argument is not unreasonable. The present value of $1 to be earned some time in the future depends on the opportunity cost associated with the investment. The amount of the yield rate or discount rate makes a big difference in the present value. It also depends on when the "rent" is to be considered as having been earned.

Assume that one side (say the DOT) opines that the $10,000 rent is earned and paid as of the end of the year, and that the appropriate opportunity cost for land rent is 10%. The other side (the condemnee) opines that mortgage rates are a reasonable proxy for the risks associated with the land and the "rent" is payable in advance, at the first of the year. The present value matrix would look as follows:

			YEAR				
			0	1	2	3	4
PRESENT-VALUE OF TEMPORARY EASEMENT; LAND RENT EXAMPLE							
DISCOUNT RATE (CONDEMNOR'S OPINION)	10%	PV FACTOR	1.000000	0.9090909	0.826446	0.751315	0.683013
DISCOUNT RATE (CONDEMNEE'S OPINION)	4%	PV FACTOR	1.000000	0.961538	0.924556	0.888996	0.854804
RENT (CONDEMNOR'S OPINION)			0	$10,000	$10,000	$10,000	$0
RENT (CONDEMNEE'S OPINION)			$10,000	$10,000	$10,000	$10,000	
ASSUME THREE-YEAR CONSTRUCTION PERIOD							
PRESENT-VALUE, CONDEMNOR'S OPINION	SUM OF PV		$24,869	$0	$9,091	$8,264	$7,513	$0
PRESENT-VALUE, CONDEMNEE'S OPINION	SUM OF PV		$28,861	$10,000	$9,615	$9,246	$8,890	$0
DIFFERENCE			$3,992					
ASSUME FOUR-YEAR CONSTRUCTION PERIOD	SUM PV		$24,869					
	SUM PV		$37,751					
DIFFERENCE			$12,882					

According to the DOT the condemnee should be paid $24,869 up front for the three year's rent, whereas the condemnee's calculation is $28,861 or a difference of $3,992 just associated with a difference of opinion about when rent is earned and the appropriate opportunity cost for land rent, or about a 15% difference just for these two factors. On the other hand, if the property owner is right, and the project will take four years rather than three years, the difference of opinion increases to $12,882, about a 300% increase in the appropriate compensation for the rent-use of the land, which is why the estimate of the time for a temporary easement makes the big difference.

Permanent Easements

When the Interstate Pipeline Transit Conglomerate, LLC wants to run an underground pipeline through your property, it only wants the use of your property, it doesn't want to own your property in fee simple. It wants you to still be responsible for mowing the grass and paying the property taxes. In the first place it probably wants a swath of your land starting about 3' under the surface for a pipe that may be up to 4' in diameter and runs for hundreds of miles. These types of properties generally do not sell on the open market, so the appraiser uses the "across the fence" method to appraise the value of the swath of land in fee simple. Once the value of the underlying fee is known, the appraiser estimates a reasonable annual rent-use for the swath, like the temporary easement assignment described above.

The biggest difference between valuing a temporary easement and a permanent easement is in the length of time the easement will remain in effect. Permanent easements mean "in perpetuity." That means that the rights of the easement holder are dominant (and the easement is often called a "dominant estate") and the rights of the original (or successive) fee owner are servient (often called a "servient estate"). Consequently, the servient estate is entitled to that land-use rental payment every year forever. Appraisers solve this type of problem by capitalizing in perpetuity.

Capitalizing is based on the observation that value (V) is equal to income (I) divided by Rate (R). IRV is appraiser mnemonic for Income is equal to Value times Rate (I=V*R) or Rate is equal to Income divided by Value (R=I/V) or Value is equal to Income divided by Rate (V=I/R). However, the only way to get the answer right is to be confident that one has the parts right. This is a whole lot easier to say than it is to do, so differences of opinion about the parts lead to big differences of opinion about the answer, especially when one is dividing a large number by a very small number to come to the biggest number in the equation (V=I/R). The smaller R is the bigger V will be.

R or Rate is really a proxy for the amount of risk associated with this transaction. A property owner granting a permanent easement to an interstate pipeline company may believe that the risk that the pipeline company would default on the payment of an annual land rent is no riskier than the company's bonds, for example, say 4%. The pipeline company may believe that the appropriate risk rate was comparable to the general real estate risk for any income-producing asset, say 8%. If the agreed to "I" or annual land rent was $10,000, a 4% R would indicate a V of $250,000. At an 8% R the V would be $125,000. This is enough of a difference of opinion that honest folks might be mad enough to go fight, even if they agreed on the value of the underlying land and agreed on the annual land-rent.

Another way of thinking about the appropriate share of the value of the underlying fee is associated with the easement is to try to answer the question "How much of the functional utility of the servient land remains to the fee owner?" Assume for a moment that the pipeline was to run through 10 acres of $10,000/acre crop land. Assume the same 10% land-use annual rental rate, or a possible "rent" of $10,000. However, in this case assume that the farmer was using only the top 1' of soil and the pipeline constituted "no-foul, no-harm" so long as the farmer could continue to grow his wheat in that field. Almost 100% of the functional utility of the land would remain with the servient fee.

Under the Federal rule for appraising in eminent domain, the value of the part taken is equal to the value of the entirety before the taking less the value of the remainder after the taking. In the "before" the farm land was worth $10,000/acre. In the "after" the value is almost $10,000/acre, say $9,500/acre to account for the unlikely circumstance that the pipeline had to be repaired once in 10 years and the repair ruined the crop in the easement during that year. The difference between the "before" and the "after" is just $500/acre, or $5,000 for the 10 acres. $5,000 is a lot smaller than either $125,000 or $250,000. In fact, as you may remember from the power pole case, the U.S. Court of Appeals ruled in that case that the right to one foot of a power pole for a cable line constituted "non-rivalrous property" and that the power companies were not entitled to any compensation when the Congress required them to permit the cable companies to attach their lines to power poles.

In about half of the states and in Federal condemnation proceedings, the condemning authority follows this "before and after" model, in which case the compensation in the above example would be limited to $5,000. In the other states, the condemnee must be paid for the part that is taken, which would at least give him a shot at the $125,000 or the $250,000 (or something in between).

Often the appraiser uses this idea of functional utility to base his appraisal on something other than capitalized rent-use.

Assume that the Department of Transportation (the dreaded Demons of Torment) condemned a 30'-wide swath along the frontage of your property "for the maintenance and preservation of slopes." This type of permanent easement often happens because the DOT has to protect the road and maintain slopes when there is a grade difference between the road and surrounding land. The original fee owner still owns the land, but now it is a 2:1 slope. The fee owner still has to pay the property taxes, but this time the DOT will mow the grass. However, the fee owner can't build on this land, can't put a fence on it to keep others out and has lost most of the functional utility of the tract. He or she can still count it towards development density and as a part of required setbacks, but that's about all. Suppose the appraiser decided that 90% of the functional utility of this acre of $100,000/acre land was lost due to the permanent easement for maintenance of slopes. His appraisal of just and adequate compensation would be $90,000 according to this theory of valuation.

There is no "right" answer to most questions concerning the value of the easement because there is no active third-party marketplace wherein easements are bought and sold. Consequently, appraisal theory is the best anyone can count on, and the "right answer" is either an answer wherein the parties agree or, since we have given up trial by combat, an answer determined by the courts.

Damages to the Remainder

The biggest difference of opinion in just and adequate compensation associated with any easement, in fact the usual cause of a big difference in the opinion of just and adequate compensation in any condemnation proceedings, is usually associated with the damage to the remaining property. Consider the situation of a convenience store that is told that it will lose access to the main road for "only three months." It is like a condemned man at a hanging who is assured that the hangman only will borrow the use of his neck for ten minutes or so. Three months later the building and pumps will still be there, but the gas station will be out-of-business. When eminent domain testimony was an active part of my practice, I carried a group of photographs of boarded-up convenience stores and gas stations that I could use to illustrate this point if I got the chance.

An easement running along the border of the property usually doesn't cause much trouble to the value of the remainder, but an easement running down the middle of the property could really affect the functional utility of the remainder. One of our more successful, unanchored shopping centers in Midtown Atlanta is built with stores along the north and south edges of the property and a 100' wide high-kV transmission line runs through the middle of the property. The developers put the parking in the easement, but this is a relatively unusual solution to what is usually a fatal encroachment for the remainder.

However, an appraiser ignores the exception to his own peril. It is very embarrassing to be sitting on the stand and opining to the "fact" that if an easement runs through the middle of the property the utility of the remainder is zero, and then to be presented with pictures of the Ansley Mall Shopping Center west of Clear Creek, which has a 250kV line running the center of the parking lot or Northlake Tower Festival Shopping Center, which has a 200' radio tower in the middle of the parking lot. Zero is very hard to defend. "Less" is better.

Chapter 21: Air Rights

Fee simple real estate rights range from the center of the earth to the top of the sky, or whatever of that column that is practical. This bundle of rights can be subdivided physically into subterranean rights, surface rights and air rights, depending on who wants what part. Several times throughout my career I have been asked to appraise a part of that column of air. I have three stories in mind that might illustrate why air rights get appraised and the appraisal problems that the appraiser must solve.

The Candler building is one of the very few 100-year-old buildings left in Atlanta. We Atlantans were so impressed by Billy Sherman's urban renewal plans in 1865 that we have been following his example ever since. If it is old in Atlanta we knock it down. Unless you like modern architecture, don't come here.

One of the very few exceptions to the rule is The Candler Building. To quote from the history section of the Candler Building webpage: *The Candler Building was built in 1906. This classical bastion of brass, marble, mahogany and Tiffany crystal was conceived of and personally developed by the Coca-Cola magnate, Asa Candler.* For the first 20 years of its life it was the tallest building in Atlanta.

As beautiful as it is, the Candler Building's floor-plan has provided a challenge to the owner's desire to remain attractive to the office rental market. The building is almost a flatiron shape at its front on Peachtree Street, flaring out in a "V" shape as it backs up to Woodruff Park.

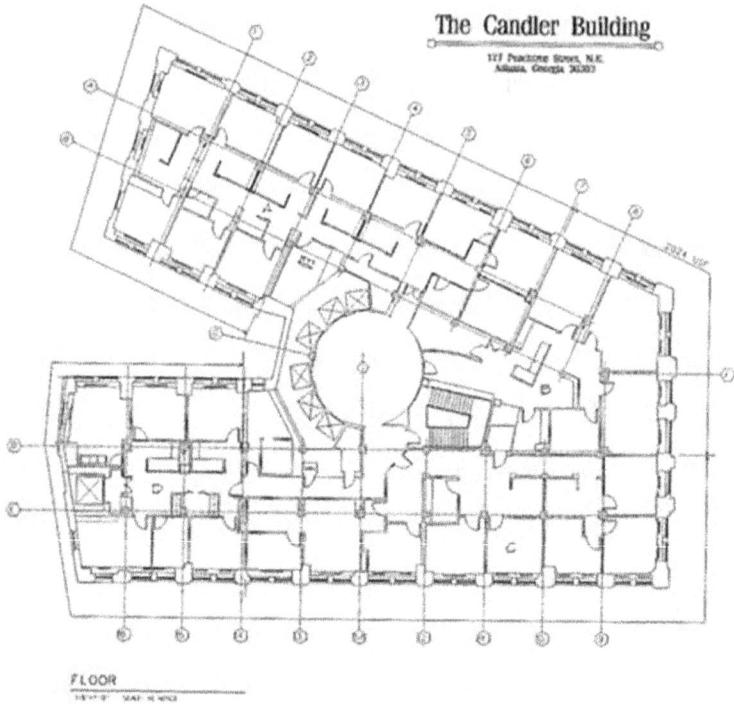

The Candler Building
117 Peachtree Street, N.E.
Atlanta, Georgia 30303

FLOOR

There is a total of 212,000 square feet of rentable space in the building, but the largest contiguous space is 20,000 sf, and many firms require much more space. One of Atlanta's prestigious law firms used to occupy 12 of the 17 stories in the Candler Building, but the lawyers found themselves spending too many billable hours just riding up and down in the elevators, and they moved to three floors of a modern office building.

About 20 years ago the building's owners developed a plan to add 40,000 sf to many of the floors by buying and building within air rights above Woodruff Park. The City of Atlanta, which owned the park, was willing to sell so long as the new addition wouldn't cast a shadow over the park, which meant acquiring the column of air from the fifth story through the 17th story. These 12 stories would add 480,000 sf of rentable space to the building, and the 60,000-sf floor-plates would accommodate many more firms, curing much of the building's functional obsolescence.

My job was to appraise the market value of this column of air. Unlike New York or other more intensely developed cities, Atlanta does not have much history with the sale of air rights. There is no readily available database of sales of air rights on which an appraiser could rely. Consequently, the sales comparison approach, which is usually the appraiser's best friend, was not available to me. The same could be said for the cost approach and the income approach. Since the Good Lord has seen fit to provide appraisers with only these three approaches I couldn't see a direct path to the solution of the appraisal problem. Fortunately, I have a somewhat devious turn of mind and I thought I could find an indirect path to the solution.

Real estate has value because it is useful. The surface and the amount of the ground below the surface that is required to build an adequate foundation are useful because they provide the space for and hold up the building that is going to be built on that ground. In an earlier story of the Midtown Plaza Shopping Center I discussed price per square foot of development density [$/sf(d)] as a unit of comparison that appraisers can use to value land suitable for commercial development. I knew that the column of air rights that had to be appraised could support a maximum of 480,000 square feet of development. I knew that generally comparable land sold for between $15/sf(d) and $20/sf(d), so the most that the air rights would be worth was between $7,200,000 and $9,600,000.

The comparable commercial land that sold for $15/sf(d) and $20/sf(d) has more utility than the air rights, because the typical $15/sf(d) or $20/sf(d) land gave the owner all the bundle of rights, not just the rights to the column of air. I knew that the appropriate appraisal would be for less than $7,200,000 to $9,600,000, which probably was the reasonable range of value for the land in fee simple. I just had to decide how much less would be reasonable.

Reasonable is all I was looking for. I thought that reasonableness could be best supported in this case by considering how a fee simple owner of the whole physical bundle of rights uses his theoretical rights to the property from the center of the earth to the heavens. About 20% of the total utility of those rights are associated with the foundation of the building, and another 10% or so with the setback and open space requirements imposed by our communities. It probably makes sense to allocate another 5% to the space below the foundation in case there are undiscovered minerals, or someone wants to run bolt holes or a deep tunnel under our building. I allocated another 5% to the air above the building in case, sometime in the future, we wanted to install a tower for the next generation dirigible or the airport wanted to acquire an avigation easement under 10,000' in elevation. That left me 60% of the total value associated with the column of air within which I could build the building.

My solution was to multiply the $/sf(d) indications by 60% to come to an answer of $9/sf(d) to $12/sf(d) for the 480,000 sf of building that could be built in the column of air rights that the Candler Building was trying to acquire from the city.

Appraisers and other reasonable people know that this craft is a judgment, not an exact science, and that often a range is a much better answer than a single-point estimator. In this case the range of the data was between $9/sf(d) and $12/sf(d), so the best answer is that the air rights were worth between $4,320,000 and $5,760,000. However, real people really don't want to know a range. They want a single number. Most of the time my readers are real people, so most of my colleagues and I give our appraisal answers in single numbers. I said that the air rights had a market value of $5,000,000.[28]

The Candler Building wasn't the only air-rights assignment I had. One of the more interesting came to me through a bond attorney who had helped one of Atlanta's prominent private schools to obtain non-taxable bonds to build a three-story building near the Northwest Expressway. One part of the IRS Regulations concerning tax-exempt bonds is that no more than 5% of the project can be involved in a non-

---

[28] Please, gentle reader, remember that all the numbers in this book are just for illustration. None reflect the actual appraisals, which remain the confidential property of the clients.

eligible form of activity or enterprise. School uses were perfectly legitimate, but the school had been approached by one of our local cell phone companies because the roof of that building would be a perfect spot for a cell array that would fill in a hole in their service. Hundreds of thousands of cars per day pass the location, and the neighbors in an affluent neighborhood really don't like cell towers in their backyard.

The school was being offered thousands of dollars a year by the cell phone company to rent the air rights and several touchdown points on the roof of the school building. The school wanted the thousands of dollars, but they couldn't jeopardize their tax-exempt status. I was asked to value the rent-use of the air rights to be sure that the amount didn't exceed the IRS's 5% limit.

In this case the amount of the bonds was approximately equal to the cost to construct the building, excluding the land. Consequently, the cost approach gave us a reasonable estimate of the contributory value of the building. My solution was to determine the share of the total cost to construct that was associated with the roof. I then applied the per square foot cost of the roof to the approximately 200 sf of roof that the cell phone company wanted to rent for their array. I applied an annual, rent-use factor reflecting both the return of and the return on the cost of that 200 sf of roof, and calculated the present value factor for the term of the proposed lease between the school and the cell phone company. Unsurprisingly, it turned out to be a lot less than the 5% limit, but the school now had a third-party appraisal to show the IRS in case of an audit.

Another air-rights assignment I found interesting involved a campus of Northside Hospital. The hospital had a six-story parking garage on top of which a group of doctors had built a six-story medical office building. The lease between the doctors and the hospital required a periodic review of the rent for the air rights occupied by the doctors' building. A periodic review meant a periodic appraisal assignment for someone, and I was fortunate to have had a reputation as an air rights appraiser.

Chapter 22: What To Do When It's Over: Retiring from an Appraisal Practice

As the lobster said, "There is no trouble getting into this trap." I drifted into this appraisal profession by good fortune when I was 45 years old, but most appraisers become appraisers when they are very young, usually because their fathers or uncles are appraisers. We are a tiny profession, and although most people have heard the name, very few have any idea about what an appraiser is or does. According to the Appraisal Institute's 2017 "Fact Sheet" there were 73,731 real estate appraisers in the U.S. in 2016, and the number is declining by about 4%/year. There are probably another 20,000 machinery and equipment, fine art and jewelry, and business appraisers in addition to the real estate appraisers, but these personal property and intangible appraisers are much more of an amorphous group who have honest jobs as jewelers or accountants or business brokers.

As we are a regulated profession the statistics are relatively easy to come by. All of us who are real estate appraisers must be registered or licensed or certified by our states, and a national registry is maintained by The Appraisal Foundation. Presently, about 78% of us have bachelor's degrees, and all new folks coming into the profession must have a four-year degree. About 57% of us are primarily certified residential appraisers, about 32% are primarily certified commercial appraisers, and 11% are newbies who are only licensed appraisers. About 22,000 of us, or a quarter, are associated with the Appraisal Institute (AI). AI members are generally considered the cream of the crop, but other professional associations, like the Royal Institute of Chartered Surveyors and the American Society of Appraisers, are very well respected. The advantage of AI membership can probably be best illustrated by the disparity in income between non-AI members and AI members. Only 29% of non-AI appraisers reported earnings above $100,000 in 2014, whereas 54% of AI members reported earnings in excess of $100,000 that same year.

Given our age distribution, the decrease in our numbers could increase precipitously over the next few years, since 62% of us were age 51 or older. Eighty-seven per cent of us are white, 75% of us are male. Consequently, if you see an old, white man driving erratically through your neighborhood paying more attention to the houses than the traffic, chances are you are looking at an appraiser.

To sum it up, we are a tiny profession of old, white men who are dying off at an alarming rate. Fifty-seven per cent of us either own our own firm or are sole proprietors. Furthermore, Zillow and other artificial intelligence algorithms threaten to replace the residential appraisers who make up the largest portion of the profession, and artificial intelligence for the commercial appraisal can't be far behind. Perhaps the only saving grace to the profession is that we can earn a pretty good living, there is no heavy lifting, and, occasionally, there is no alternative to an appraiser's opinion when there is a dispute about the value of something.

Eventually, we all grow old and start thinking about retirement. I have spent the past 20 years trying to avoid Jim Pritchett's retirement system, which was work, work, work, work, die. Unfortunately, most of my colleagues have signed up for Jim's approach. I, however, have a pressing desire to see as much of this world as I can before I leave it. Since I retired from Pritchett, Ball and Wise, Inc., in 2007, I have been to 20 countries and there are many more on the list. Since my present wife, Shelley, retired from school teaching in 2015, we have been able to extend our trips to between six weeks and three months at a single stretch. I still keep my hand in, testifying about every other month and consulting where I can be useful, but now my job is retirement, and appraisal is an avocation.

Because so many of us work as solo practitioners or in very small firms, retirement planning is generally not a part of our thinking. 401K plans and IRAs are hard to fund when the wolf is at the door or you have to make payroll. Most of us learned about the power of compound interest too late in life to make it a useful tool for us. Consequently, working until one dies appears to be a reasonable plan for many of us.

Appraisers, particularly commercial real estate appraisers, are experts on the time value of money. I cannot add anything to our general wisdom that we should pay ourselves first, put away a little each month, and let the power of compound interest carry us to our inevitable reward in some comfort. However, in addition to this general wisdom that we all know and seldom follow, I do have two ideas that stood me in good stead that probably apply to many professions in addition to appraisal.

The first is not to be a sole practitioner. Appraisal, law, accountancy and many other professions are often judgment trades wherein the professional's judgment is the most valuable service that is being provided to the client. Good professional judgments are seldom best made alone. Someone has to do the research and the heavy thinking, but someone else should review the work to see the obvious flaws that are invisible to the primary author. It is far better to have your business partner and colleague find the critical error of fact or judgment than to discover it under cross-examination in court. You can't depend on your spouse or a friend to be knowledgeable enough and have enough invested in your common reputation to show you where you are being a damned fool. That level of honesty is the responsibility of your partner, so you'd better have one.

Partners are hard to come by. Sometimes someone with whom you have gone through the professional training and certification or designation process becomes a friend and is a good fit for a partner. Sometimes, along the way you will find a colleague ready for a change with whom you may partner to form a new firm. The best way, in my opinion, is to grow a partner by hiring every young associate you hire with the intention that he or she will grow to become your partner over the next 10 to 15 years and eventually they will buy you out. That brings me to my best retirement advice. Plan to be bought out by your partners.

After I had obtained my MAI designation, about three years into my employment, Jim Pritchett and Joe Ball asked me to become a partner in the firm. During that process I learned that PBW, Inc., had not done a lot of thinking about the firm as a business. As is the case in most small appraisal firms, the stockholders, Jim and Joe, were first and foremost appraisers, not businessmen. By then, I had already qualified to become a business appraiser and had appraised a number of small firms, so I had some idea of what drove value in a small professional practice. I asked for a couple of things that stood me in good stead twenty years later when I retired.

The first was that I asked that we have the firm appraised by an independent professional. I know, appraisers actually finding an appraisal useful is a shocking concept, but, if for no other reason than to humor me, my about-to-be partners agreed, and we paid for a business appraisal of PBW, Inc. The appraisal became the foundation for all the future company events that relied on a valuation of the firm. I don't mean to say that the actual number that our business appraiser came up with mattered in the future. That number in fact only mattered in the immediate transaction at hand, which was my buy-in. The real long-term benefit of the appraisal was in our understanding of the methods that the business appraiser applied to come up with the value of our firm. When it came to those future events that required a valuation of our stock, such as at Jim's death or George's buying-in or my retirement, we used those methods and techniques to update our value considerations.

The second thing that I asked for was that we buy whole life, key man insurance to back up the value of the stock. Having key-man insurance is critical to the life of a firm. In our case, Jim Pritchett was my rainmaker. I had just turned 50, and Jim was 11 years older than I was. Joe, who is about five years younger than I am, had been with Jim for almost 20 years by the time I bought in, and Joe had a good client base and an established practice, but Joe didn't particularly like court work. I, on the other hand, was just breaking in as a litigation support appraiser. I very much needed Jim's reputation and relationship with the attorneys if I was going to be successful. Our key-man insurance policy on Jim's life had to be big enough to make it possible to continue to run the firm long enough for me to sell myself to the litigation marketplace in the event he were to die or become disabled.

Another benefit of the appraisal was that it forced us to recognize and expressly deal with the fact that the value of stock in small, privately held firms faces two types of discounts not associated with publicly traded stock. The first is a discount for lack of control. The second is a discount for lack of marketability. Each of these discounts can be substantial, and they are additive, which is why a minority block of stock in a small, privately held company sells for much less than a controlling block, and any share sells for less than it would if it were a share in a similar but publicly traded company.

To pay attention to these two realities about our company, we determined in our buy-sell agreement that no single partner would own a controlling block of shares, and at the event of a sale, we would ignore the lack of control discount. We further agreed, that should a partner (stockholder) resign or retire, we would apply the lack of marketability discount for any shares in excess of the cash surrender value of that partner's key-man insurance policy. We further agreed that upon death, to the extent that the value of the shares was backed up by the insurance policy, we would ignore both discounts.

Jim lived another 13 years, and I was able to work under his tutelage and friendship. I was truly fortunate to have had him as my mentor, and my memory of Jim still serves me as a compass. When Jim did die, the key-man insurance policy on his life made it possible for the firm to buy his stock from his widow, Fancy. After all, the stock is an intangible. The stock certificate is just a piece of paper. Our small firm would have had the obligation to buy Fancy's inherited stock, but absent the insurance proceeds would not have had the means. We were a reasonably successful firm, but we didn't have over a hundred thousand dollars in cash lying around. The insurance policy meant that the stock really had value.

The whole life component of our key-man insurance came into play when I decided to retire in 2007. Whole life insurance includes a buildup of equity, as well as death benefits. PBW, Inc. didn't have any big pile of cash lying around when I retired, but my key-man insurance policy had built up enough cash surrender value to make it possible for the firm to buy back more than half of my stock. I took a 10-year note for the balance of my stock, and the monthly payments were not an onerous burden on the firm's cash flow, although I heard that the remaining partners threw a celebration once they had made the final payment.

The reason that stock in small firms doesn't have value is that there is very seldom a market for the shares. Most of the real value in a professional service firm is tied up in personal goodwill, and most of the cash flow over third-party operating expenses goes to the owners, either in a salary that they set for themselves or in profits. That is why so many of these small firms are structured as Sub S corporations or LLCs. These are called "pass-through" entities for a good reason.

When you buy into a firm, particularly as a minority shareholder, all you are doing is committing yourself to those partners and that firm with a self-imposed set of financial handcuffs. The only way out is to earn your buy-in back, partially based on the reputation of the firm; live long enough for the cash surrender value of your key-man life insurance policy to grow to the point that your stock has enough value to at least repay the principal on your original investment; or die. Buying into a firm is very much like committing to a marriage. The financial handcuffs are very useful when you and your partners bump into the same sorts of personality clashes or disagreements that are also part of a marriage. Your stock shares are much like your wedding ring. They remind you that you are committed to each other, not just to your clients and to the work you do as an individual professional.

Now I am 10 years retired. One of the nicest things I have learned is that I have been able to keep my fingers in the appraisal world as a consultant and occasionally as an expert witness or as a rebuttal witness on cases that interest me. These days I generally affiliate myself with a much younger appraiser who has access to and familiarity with all the modern data services and is willing to do all of the heavy lifting of finding the comparables. I think and opine and am still believable in court. I now have the time to make it possible for my wife and me to travel. Retirement's greatest blessing has been to permit me to have more control over my time.

Chapter 23: Summing Up a Career

Much of my career of the past 35 years has been the result of luck. As a political science college instructor, and later staff to the Georgia Municipal Association, I had learned useful things about the management and administration of cities and counties. These things made me useful to cities and counties trying to negotiate the vagaries of the grant-in-aid business as the Department of Housing and Urban Development (HUD) was transitioning from silo grants to community development block grants (CDBG) and cities and counties had to compete for limited funds. I was able to help my clients put a thumb on the scale and win the money that they wanted for a new firehouse or a water line or a sewer pond. Often, for smaller jurisdictions wherein the amount of the grant was as big as or bigger than the typical year's budget for the city, I would administer the grant to make sure that the work got done and that no Federal regulations were broken. I only had one client go to jail, and that was for a failure in judgment not associated with any of my grants.

As the HUD's CDBG program matured, cities and counties began to compete for economic development funds as well as grants for infrastructure. I went back to school for a master of science degree in economics studying urban economics and micro economics so I could continue to be useful. I have always felt more comfortable peddling advice when I have a reasonably solid academic foundation to support my opinions. My clients tried attracting industries by constructing industrial parks and two- or three-sided building shells as bait. After a while I also worked with industries that were trying to get the local government to do something to improve the industry's position or solve some zoning or infrastructure problem.

I drifted into appraisal when I learned that I didn't know enough about real estate to continue my earlier profession of selling advice to local governments.

As time went by I found myself more in the real estate business than the political science or economics business. Real estate developers are in the supply side of the business, and I have never met a developer who wasn't certain that the market would swoop down and gobble up all the space that he had created in his new development as soon as the concrete had cured and the paint had dried. By then the banking regulations had changed sufficiently to require that commercial real estate appraisers had to undertake substantive market analysis to support the concept that a new shopping center or new apartment complex would be absorbed by the market before the developer could get his construction loan approved. Remember, these were the good old days when bankers were concerned about collateral for their loans, before the financial engineers created credit-default swaps and other inventive "alternative securities."

I started getting calls from commercial appraisers to subcontract the market analysis portion of their reports. I didn't know that there was such a thing as a commercial real estate appraiser. I only knew of residential appraisers, and only because they were a part of my having bought a couple of houses along the years. Once I started working with a few of the commercial appraisal firms and saw the magnitude of research that went into their appraisal reports I became impressed. I had the good fortune to have been introduced to Jack Goldstucker, Ph.D., who chaired the marketing department at Georgia State University's College of Business Administration. Jack told me that GSU had a real estate department that offered degrees through the Ph.D. in real estate. I thought that my future might be enough embroiled in real estate to enroll.

At GSU I met and studied under Jim Vernor, Ph.D, Joe Rabianski, Ph.D., Julian Diaz, Ph.D., and many others who since have become friends and colleagues. Over the years I have employed all these great folks as contractors on various projects. Between 1984 and 2000 I took almost all the coursework in real estate available at GSU and was awarded the Graduate Certificate in Real Estate in 2001.

In January of 1984 I went to my first meeting of the Atlanta Chapter of the American Institute of Real Estate Appraisers (AIREA), one of the two predecessor organizations that currently make up the Appraisal Institute. Waiting for the meeting to start I sat next to a pretty lady at the bar who introduced herself as Fancy Pritchett, and Fancy told me that I had to meet her husband, Jim.

Meeting Jim Pritchett was the second truly important part of my good-luck story. Jim was one of the nation's best-respected appraisers whose work primarily involved testifying about his opinions in court. Before the merger of the AIREA and the Society of Appraisers to form the Appraisal Institute, Jim had earned designation from both prior organizations, and had been President of the Atlanta chapters of each. He was an original member of the Appraisal Foundation Qualifications Board (AQB), and, following his death in 2002, the Appraisal Institute established the James H. Pritchett Award.

Jim had been a ballet dancer with the Atlanta Ballet, a submariner (retired as a Captain in the Navy), and a founding member of the Atlanta Lawn Tennis Association (ALTA), which is one of the largest amateur sports leagues in the U.S. With Jim I got to appraise Water Island, the fourth largest island in the U.S. Virgin Islands, the Everglades and the Big Cypress, mines and wells, a grease-and-tallow factory and dozens of other unusual properties. Going to work every day was an adventure, and I never got bored. Because I was lucky enough to follow Jim into litigation-support appraisal, I had a career made up of unusual properties and unusual circumstances. These assignments gave me the stories that gave me a chance to illustrate how an appraiser thinks about value even when the property type and/or the specific interest to be appraised are out of the ordinary.

The day before Jim died, Charles Pursley, Esq., his long-time colleague and friend, and I were with him when he offered the following prayer:

"Dear God,

Thank you for giving me a life in which I could use my knowledge, skills, and judgment to do useful work for people at times in their lives when my judgment mattered. Thank you for calling on me to act responsibly and to tell the truth."

—JIM PRITCHETT, January 24, 2002.

I still don't know of a better benediction for my profession.

Table of Abbreviations

AI: The Appraisal Institute.

AIREA: American Institute of Real Estate Appraisal (predecessor organization for the Appraisal Institute).

APB: The Appraisal Practice Board of the Appraisal Foundation.

AQB: The Appraisal Qualifications Board of the Appraisal Foundation.

ASB: The Appraisal Standards Board of The Appraisal Foundation.

CAP: The capitalization rate.

CAPM: The Capital Asset Pricing Model.

CATV: Community Antenna Television.

CBA: Certified Business Appraiser designation from the Institute of Business Appraisers.

CCRC: Continuing Care Retirement Community.

CFA: Chartered Financial Analyst.

CON: Certificate of Need.

D.O.T.: Department of Transportation. Sometimes G.D.O.T. for the Georgia Department of Transportation.

EBITDA: Earnings before Interest, Taxes, Depreciation, Amortization.

FASB: Financial Accounting Standards Board.

FIRREA: Financial Institution Reform, Recovery and Enforcements Act (1989).

GCRE: Graduate Certificate in Real Estate.

HPA: Health Planning Agency.

IBA: Institute of Business Appraisers. This formerly independent organization, which was the oldest in the profession, was acquired by the National Association of Certified Valuation Analysts (NACVA).

M&E: Machinery and Equipment.

MAI: Designates the senior level of minimum training and competence for a commercial property appraiser. The initials currently have no particular meaning. Formerly they designated a Member of the American Institute.

NACVA: National Association of Certified Valuation Analysts.

NAICS: North American Industry Classification System.

NOI: Net Operating Income.

RM: Former designation of the AIREA for a Residential Member.

ROW: Right of Way.

SME: Subject Matter Experts who advise the APB.

SRA: Society of Real Estate Appraisers. Presently the residential designation for members of the AI. Used to refer to a predecessor organization for the Appraisal Institute.

SRPA: Former designation of the SRA for a Senior Real Property Appraiser.

USPAP: The Uniform Standards of Professional Appraisal Practice .

WACC: The Weighted Average Cost of Capital.

www.ingramcontent.com/pod-product-compliance
Lightning Source LLC
Chambersburg PA
CBHW071559210326
41597CB00019B/3316